What people are saying about

BETTER THAN YOU CAN IMAGINE

"If you're a compulsive creative like me, knowing your gift and how to use it for the kingdom is often difficult to understand. Patrick, an amazing pastor and dear friend of mine, delivers a simple but profound message, encouraging us to walk through this life aware of our gifts and of how beautiful and fulfilling it is to give them away."

Mark Stuart, two-time Grammy Award winner with Audio Adrenaline and cofounder of the Hands and Feet Project

"This book is a must read for anyone who has ever questioned their value in the kingdom of God. In this book, pastor and author Patrick Quinn outlines four principles that will help you focus and build on the gift that God has given you. His observational style of writing brings you right alongside him in the journey. You will be both encouraged and empowered to start using your God-given gifts to be a blessing."

Joe Amaral, pastor, teacher, and author of *Understanding Jesus*

"I have become a close friend of Patrick Quinn and love his service to our God. We have had long talks of how the Holy Spirit has directed his life and the joy that brings. This powerful book reminds us that God has a way of giving everybody something. What He gives does not belong to us but it belongs to the kingdom. And every day we are being asked, 'Who is on the Lord's side?' As Levi said, 'I am.' We have to take our gifts and minister to others to show 'I am.' Therefore, read this book, do what it instructs, and find peace."

Dr. Kevin Elko, "head" (mental) coach of
the Alabama Crimson Tide football team

"Patrick Quinn implores us to explore our God-given gifts, focus on going deeper with them, and see the need to be in community with other Christ followers. *Better Than You Can Imagine* is a great read filled with stories of people from all walks of life who once could only imagine the wonderful places God has now placed them."

Bishop David Graves, resident bishop
of the Alabama-West Florida Conference
of the United Methodist Church

"There is no question that God has positioned His people—in just the right places, with just the right gifts—to bring His healing and redemption to the world. *Better Than You Can Imagine* will help us understand our gifts, see the needs around us, and unlock the joy that comes when we experience God's true purpose for our lives."

Brad Johnson, president and CEO
of Mission of Hope Haiti

"So much of life is our attitude. Trusting in God's divine plan for us enhances our attitude unbelievably. Patrick Quinn describes it as 'better than you can imagine.' The real joy of life comes when we discover our gift and let God use it to do His work and meet the needs of others. Get ready to stretch your vision and enjoy life at a new level as you put Patrick's suggestions into practice."

Dr. John Ed Mathison, retired senior minister of Frazer United Methodist Church

"With the gentleness of a good storyteller, Quinn uses his family's foster-parenting saga to capture us up in the reality that we are also actors in the same adventure. He guides us through a framework of promises: discovering our Life Gift, offering it to needs that only we can relationally meet, and the joy (and frustration) that comes along the way. My ministry is under full reimagination after this reading."

Dr. Daryl L. Smith, EdD, associate professor of Mentored Ministry and Christian Leadership at Asbury Theological Seminary and author of *The End of Small Groups*

"I have always admired Patrick Quinn as an excellent writer and speaker. In his latest book, Patrick focuses on discerning our unique gifts and matching those gifts with the needs of others. Let me recommend Patrick's book to you in hopes that you will discover that joy and happiness are never found in material things, but rather in using our unique gifts to lovingly serve others."

Dr. Karl Stegall, retired minister of First United Methodist Church and president of Stegall Seminary Scholarship Endowment Foundation

"This book will light a fuse that won't go out and will keep on burning for a lifetime. You might call it 'Great Balls of Fire' for the soul."

Leonard Sweet, bestselling author, professor at Drew University, George Fox University, and Tabor College, and founder of The Story Lectionary and www.preachthestory.com

"Patrick Quinn is an emerging talented writer who has the unusual ability to describe life lessons in an engaging way that inspires, endears, and instructs. In *Better Than You Can Imagine*, Patrick uses his own experience as a pastor and foster parent to unpack four transformative life keys that unlock God's story in our lives. Simple, but profound, this is a guide book for the adventure called *life*."

Jim Tomberlin, pastor, founder and CEO of MultiSite Solutions, and coauthor of *Better Together*

BETTER
THAN
YOU
CAN
IMAGINE

GOD'S CALLING, YOUR ADVENTURE

BETTER THAN YOU CAN IMAGINE

PATRICK M. QUINN with KEN ROACH

David C Cook®

transforming lives together

BETTER THAN YOU CAN IMAGINE
Published by David C Cook
4050 Lee Vance Drive
Colorado Springs, CO 80918 U.S.A.

David C Cook U.K., Kingsway Communications
Eastbourne, East Sussex BN23 6NT, England

The graphic circle C logo is a registered trademark of David C Cook.

The website addresses recommended throughout this book are offered as a
resource to you. These websites are not intended in any way to be or imply an
endorsement on the part of David C Cook, nor do we vouch for their content.

Details in some stories have been changed to protect
the identities of the persons involved.

Bible credits are listed at the back of this book.
The author has added italics to Scripture quotations for emphasis.

LCCN 2017931156
ISBN 978-0-7814-1298-8
eISBN 978-1-4347-1149-6

© 2017 Patrick M. Quinn with Ken Roach

The Team: Alice Crider, LB Norton, Amy Konyndyk, Nick Lee,
Melanie Larson, Abby DeBenedittis, Susan Murdock
Cover Design: James Hershberger
Cover Photo: Getty Images

Printed in the United States of America

First Edition 2017

1 2 3 4 5 6 7 8 9 10

032917

For every child that calls our house their home,
you make our lives better than you can imagine.
We pray the same will be for each of you!
—Patrick (and Rachael)

For Ronan James Fedor, my first
grandchild. I pray that your future will
be better than anyone can imagine!
—Ken

CONTENTS

ACKNOWLEDGMENTS

This is a book about finding God's adventure for your life by investing in the needs of others. The content of this book is the culmination of my life adventure with Jesus that has taken me to the highest mountaintops and the lowest valleys. Over the years, I've been overwhelmingly blessed by those who invested in me as part of their own adventure with God.

I am so thankful for my wife, Rachael, who said yes! Yes to marrying me, yes to ministry, and yes to foster care. I am thankful to my children, Kaylee, Patrick, and Cate, who loved every vulnerable child who entered our home and taught me so much about loving the strangers among us. I owe a debt of gratitude to my parents and grandparents for the love, support, and encouragement I have always received. Moreover, a special mention to my grandpa Bob and stepfather, Mac, two men who never had biological children but loved the children in their homes as if they were their very own. I learned from them that family is much more than a biological connection.

I am thankful for organizations that I have been blessed to work alongside, including the United Methodist Children's Home, the Alabama Department of Human Resources, the Mission of Hope Haiti, and the Hands and Feet Project, which work tirelessly to care for orphaned and vulnerable children. I have benefited from being in close proximity to some amazing people who work every day on behalf of the children in their care.

Ken Roach, my coauthor, contributed enormously to creating this book that encapsulates my heart for people to experience the adventure of Jesus. Formed through a collaboration that brought our unique gifts to the table, this book demonstrates the very principles we seek to teach.

James Keith Posey, a longtime friend in the ministry, helped cast our vision for the content in this book. More importantly, his encouragement to share what God has uniquely put inside me is an incredible source of energy.

Finally, I thank God for my calling into ministry. I was a lost soul moving in a direction far from the path of eternal life, but God wasn't finished with me yet. Thank you, Jesus, for the abundant life found in your saving grace. Thank you, Jesus, for the incredible calling to follow you!

When I was a child, my mother hung a poster in my room that said, "Life is 10% what happens to you and 90% how you choose to react to it." Unfortunately, over the years I have seen many people fall into the trap of living as if just the opposite were true, allowing their circumstances to define them and missing out on God's calling for them. I'm thankful for my mom's message and for those who have come alongside me through the years to help me embrace its truth. My prayer is that this book will be used by the Holy Spirit to nudge others toward this life that is "better than you can imagine." Your adventure is waiting!

Chapter 1

BETTER THAN I
COULD IMAGINE

My journey started the summer of 2009 when my wife, Rachael, saw a billboard advertising the need for foster families. She looked over at me and said, "We should do that." I looked back at her and said, "We really shouldn't do that!"

From time to time over the next several years, Rachael brought up the idea of becoming a foster family, but I was resistant. Sometimes I would see a distraught look on her face, so I would ask, "Honey, what's bothering you?" She would answer, "I'm just sitting here thinking how we are not answering the call to care for orphans." Ouch.

You have to understand, my wife is not a nag; she doesn't complain or criticize me on a regular basis. On the contrary, she's my biggest supporter. Yet the burden to care for these children was only growing on her with each passing day. I had seen that look in her eyes before; it's the look of someone being called by God. And I knew in my heart that it wasn't my wife's voice I was shutting out—it was God's.

By that stage of my life, I was familiar with God's unexpected callings. When I was a child, my grandmother said I was her "preacher boy," called by the Lord to the Christian ministry. That sounded ridiculous through my wild teenage and college years, and I told my grandmother so. I believed vaguely in God, but I didn't believe in Jesus. The idea of a God who became human seemed far-fetched to me. And even if Jesus were real, I was pretty sure He wouldn't want someone like me to be a preacher. But gradually, graciously, in subtle and surprising ways, God drew me back to Him. As my heart began to warm to His mysterious but real presence, my faith was awakened, and I became a follower of Jesus. Most surprising, I began to feel a stirring of desire to share this transformation with others. I didn't feel worthy or equipped to be a pastor, but that didn't seem to matter to God. While the journey into the ministry would take many years of education and training, the first stop was to apologize to my grandmother, who had been right all along. You have to watch out for those praying grandmas!

Nevertheless, my wife's insistence that our family was called by God to foster fell on deaf ears. I had too many good, rational reasons why fostering children would be a bad idea. Of course, in theory I believed in the importance of caring for the orphan, the poor and needy, the most vulnerable among us—people whom Jesus called "the least of these." I even preached about how Jesus taught "whatever you did for one of the least of these brothers and sisters of mine, you did for me" (Matt. 25:40 NIV). But Rachael and I already had three children of our own. We weren't independently wealthy. Foster care sounded complicated and messy. So I continued telling Rachael and the Holy Spirit no.

Then one day in 2011, as I was sitting on the beach, minding my own business, God finally broke through to me.

A BEACH BECOMES A BURNING BUSH

It was a beautiful morning on the Gulf Coast of Florida. The white-sand beaches colliding with the emerald waters of the Gulf of Mexico created a picture-perfect scene. I grew up around these beaches, and they always bring me back to a place of peace. The sun was shining, the wind was singing, and the steady roar of the ocean filled my ears like an enchanting drumbeat of peace and relaxation. My children, Kaylee, Patrick Wilson, and Cate, were all building sand castles with plastic buckets we had brought from home. Rachael was sitting in a beach chair next to me, enjoying a book. I was soaking up the view of the perfect family vacation.

In an instant, this perfect scene with the sun shimmering and the ocean waves dancing stood still. It was as if everything went silent. Three children were playing, but there were four buckets. Three buckets full of sand, full of play, full of life. One bucket lying on its side, unused. Somehow, that empty bucket called to me. It spoke to me of possibility, of opportunity, of abundance: we had more resources available than I had realized. And somewhere there was a child who could be playing with that bucket, enjoying the sunshine, feeling the breeze, and hearing the ocean. The bucket spoke to me of longing and desire: caring for another child might not be just a duty; it might be a delight. We already had a spare bucket. We just needed the child to play with it.

That empty bucket became like Moses's burning bush for me. Moses heard God's voice saying, "This is holy ground," and then God sent him on a mission to rescue His people from slavery in Egypt. The beach that day became a place where I heard God's voice calling. A place where I was given a special assignment that would completely change the trajectory of my life. A place where I was sent on a mission to rescue some children in need. And a place where I encountered the presence of God in an unforgettable new way. I too was on holy ground.

BACK TO BABY MODE

Rachael and I started down the long checklist of tasks necessary to be certified by the Alabama Department of Human Resources (DHR) as foster parents. We filled out forms, attended weeks of training classes, procured character references, and opened up our home to be studied. Altogether, it took about nine months. It was work, but we considered it well worth the investment. We were convinced this was God's call for our lives, to provide a temporary home for children who needed us.

Finally the day arrived, and a beautiful eight-week-old baby boy came to live with us. We were scared. We looked at each other as if to say, *What have we done?* Of course, with three children of our own, we knew about caring for a baby, but this was different. We had taken a little stranger into our home. We did not know his family or his situation. We did not know what he liked or didn't like. All we knew was to do our best to love Timothy[1] as though he were our own child. And so we did.

We went back to baby mode. Back to baby strollers and car seats, back to changing diapers, washing bottles, and rocking an infant at midnight. Everything had to be baby-proofed again: outlets covered, gates put up, breakables moved to the top shelves. We were reminded that when a baby is in the house, the baby is in charge!

We could see how every aspect of our lives had been turned upside down, but we could also see the benefits. Our children helped in so many ways: Kaylee, who was sixteen at the time, did a lot of babysitting. Patrick, seven, became our "gopher," fetching anything we needed from all over the house when our hands were full with Timothy. Caitlin, five, loved having a little brother to play with and look after. Having a foster child gave new purpose to our family and helped form character in our children. Our whole family was beginning to live on mission for Christ inside our own home. Even the way our children said their prayers changed, shifting from purely personal requests to often praying on behalf of their new brother. We grew as a family, not only numerically but spiritually.

We had the privilege of witnessing many of the "firsts" during Timothy's first year of life. We delighted in seeing him grow and develop and flourish in new ways. We did everything in our power to make sure he was getting the best start in life possible. Over fourteen months, he went from being a stranger to becoming a part of our family. Simply put, we fell in love.

BECOMING FAMILY

At the end of our season with him, Timothy was no longer just a foster child. In our hearts and minds, he became our son. Of course, we knew from the beginning this was a temporary situation. For his own sake, we hoped and longed for the day when his biological parents would be in a position to bring him back into their own home. We had opportunities to meet and get to know them. They loved him dearly and wanted to raise him. That was a beautiful thing!

You see, that baby boy taught me that family is so much more than what we often think. Biological connections are not the only bonds that make a family; there are also "Christological connections." According to the Scriptures, when a person becomes a Christian, he or she becomes part of Christ's "body," sharing in His identity. So, when you are in Christ, God's family becomes your family. "Now all of us can come to the Father through the same Holy Spirit because of what Christ has done for us," wrote Paul. "So now you ... are no longer strangers and foreigners. You are citizens along with all of God's holy people. You are members of God's family" (Eph. 2:18–19).

Our foster baby is part of God's family. His parents are part of God's family. That means this baby and his parents are my family too. They are my brother and sister in Christ. This baby and his parents share the same blood that I do: the blood of Jesus, shed on the cross. They say blood is thicker than water, but the bond of the blood of Christ is thicker than both!

THE PROMISES OF THE ADVENTURE

In order to see God's vision in your life and become part of God's story, there are three promises you must claim. They are true for everyone, everywhere. We'll unpack them in detail in this book, specifically in the next three chapters, but here they are in a nutshell:

> **1. You have a *gift* only you can give.** Right now, already in your possession, you have a little extra—a resource, a talent, an asset, a gift—ready to be given. You are blessed. You can be a blessing.
>
> **2. Someone has a *need* only you can meet.** There is a problem, an issue, a hurt, a wound somewhere in the world that only you can heal, no matter how inadequate you may feel.

3. Joy is the *journey* where the gift and the need collide. Your inner satisfaction, your ultimate fulfillment, your life purpose, your true happiness will never be fully unlocked until your unique gift and the world's unique need come together. God's path for your life is a collision course; the intersection where your gift crashes into the world's need is where you will truly begin to live.

Those three simple promises—the gift, the need, the journey—are the secret to opening your eyes to God's vision. They are the keys that will begin to unlock God's story in your life. They will transform an ordinary life into an extraordinary adventure.

Does that seem too neat and tidy to you? Do you think it sounds too good to be true? Honestly, it *is* too simple. Those three promises are indeed the beginning, but in order to tell the whole story, I need to add a fourth promise of the adventure:

4. The journey will break you ... but it will also make you.

We will unpack this fourth promise more in a later chapter. I don't pretend that following God's callings means nothing but happiness and sunshine. It didn't mean that for Jesus, and it doesn't mean that for us. However, just as Christ's path led Him through the cross to the resurrection, so the pain we experience in following God's adventure leads us to true, abundant life.

LIVING THE PROMISES

Looking back, I can see how the first promise of the adventure was true for us. Staring at an extra sand bucket that day left me pondering one major question: *Do I have enough room in my heart?* Despite all my rational arguments to the contrary, we had room in our home for another child. We had a seat at our table, a spot in our van, a bed under our roof, margin in our budget, time in our schedule, and yes, room in our hearts. We just had to be willing to give it.

I can also see the second promise: our foster son had a need that only we could meet at that moment in time. Through no fault of his own, Timothy found himself completely vulnerable and helpless and in a position where his father and mother could not care for him. If no one had answered the call to provide a home, he would have had nowhere to go. The DHR had already made eight phone calls before calling us.

As for the third promise, there is no doubt that I encountered joys along the journey with our first foster child that I would never have experienced otherwise. I had a great marriage, good children, and a happy home. I wasn't "missing" anything. Nevertheless, I found a treasure by opening my heart. Each moment with him, even the difficult ones, became a new joy. My personal joy was exponentially multiplied by seeing the same joy on the faces of my wife and children and by knowing how much each of us was growing through this experience.

YOU ARE THE BUCKET

You see, the plastic toy bucket I saw in the sand that day wasn't the only container that needed to be filled. The true empty bucket was *me*. God wanted to fill up the empty room in my heart with a little more of Himself, so that I could pour more of His love out into the world. In the process of being filled up and then emptied out, somehow I became fuller still.

I experienced this prayer: "So that Christ may dwell in your hearts through faith—that you, being rooted and grounded in love, may have strength to comprehend with all the saints what is the breadth and length and height and depth, and to know the love of Christ that surpasses knowledge, that you may be *filled* with all the *fullness* of God" (Eph. 3:17–19 ESV).

My prayer is that I will continue to find more empty buckets in my life, more ways that I can be the container for God's fullness and blessing. We have taken other foster children into our home since then and plan for more in the future. And we've found other ways to give, other missions to be a part of, other needs to meet. Each time, our hearts get opened a little more, stretched a little more, broken a little more, but also filled with God's goodness and love a little more.

WHO THIS STORY IS ABOUT

This book is a story about me, but it's really a story about you. I want to tell you more about my adventure with foster care, but more than that, I want to help you discover your own adventure. I'll also be sharing with you the stories of others who have discovered meaning, purpose, and joy in the most unexpected journeys. And in doing so, I hope to help you discover the meaning, purpose, and joy of your own unexpected journey with God. I want you to encounter *your* burning bush … and see if you too might have an extra bucket on your beach. I know that when you hear and respond to God's calling, the adventure that follows will be better than you can imagine.

In my experience as a pastor, I've found that God often appears to people in unexpected ways. The Spirit doesn't always look the way we thought God's presence would look. After all, nobody recognized Jesus when He came: "He came into the very world he created, but the world didn't recognize him" (John 1:10). Those who did recognize Him were often those who started off blind but had their eyes opened by His touch. That's my desire for you: to receive a vision of God's kingdom. To have your eyes opened to the presence of the Holy Spirit all around you.

The story of God is made up of millions of individual stories: lives just like yours, transformed by hearing His call, seeing His vision, and feeling His touch. Even the Bible, God's uniquely revealed Word, is filled with stories—stories of imperfect, ordinary, everyday people who answered the call of Jesus: "Come, follow Me." Kings and warriors, farmers and fishermen, princesses and prostitutes, old women and little boys—their stories were turned upside down when they bumped up against the kingdom of heaven and let it get hold of them. They changed the world because something changed them.

That's how God's story continues to go out today. People ignore the Bible every day; to them, it's just a book. But they have a hard time ignoring the "living Bibles"—Christ followers who have been radically altered by a touch from heaven. We get to be a part of God's unfolding story in the world, a chapter in God's good news, if we have eyes to see and ears to hear.

SEEING THE OCEAN AGAIN FOR THE FIRST TIME

Someone asked Rachael what memories stand out to her the most from our initial journey into foster care. She immediately thought of the day that we returned to the beach for another family vacation, only this time with four children instead of three. She remembers walking into our room and opening the blinds onto the balcony, allowing our foster son to see the vastness of the ocean. It was a sight he might never have seen if he had not been placed with us. His eyes got huge, his jaw dropped, and he was speechless.

In that moment we were seeing the ocean again for the first time, through his eyes. More than that, we were seeing the ocean of God's love. The world is so much fuller than we realize. God has so much more to give us than we allow. Our narrow, restricted hearts need to be stretched and strained and broken and remade to hold it all in. As the song "How He Loves" says, "If His grace is an ocean, we're all sinking."[2]

I could have stayed in my familiar, comfortable, pre-foster-care world forever. I could have sat and watched the ocean for years on end and never see it the way I saw it through my foster son's eyes. I could have left that empty bucket empty.

God, my God, keep filling the empty buckets of my life with Your love. Do it again, Jesus. Do it again!

DISCUSSION QUESTIONS

1. Do you remember the first time you saw the ocean? What was it like? Or, if you've never visited the ocean, what do you imagine it would be like?

2. Who do you identify with the most in Patrick's story of becoming a foster parent, and why?

- Patrick—resisting God's call to move out of his comfort zone
- Rachael—trying to get someone else on board for a new adventure
- Their foster son—in a difficult situation and hoping someone will reach out to help him
- Their other children—along for the ride, not sure how all this is going to affect them yet

3. Remember the Spirit doesn't always look the way we thought God's presence would look. After all, nobody recognized Jesus when He came. Has God ever shown up in a way that you didn't recognize at first? How did it change you? How did it change your understanding of God?

4. When Timothy saw the ocean for the first time, Patrick's whole family saw the ocean for the first time again, through his eyes.

More than that, they were seeing the ocean of God's love. How much of God's love would you say you are currently experiencing? Discuss why you agree or disagree with this statement: "We cannot fully experience God's love for us until we see it from the perspective of someone else's eyes."

Chapter 2

———————

YOU HAVE A GIFT
ONLY YOU CAN GIVE

Let's take a trip back in time to the Old Testament. Here we meet a woman who literally had less than nothing. She not only had no money, but she was deeply in debt, far more than she could ever pay back. And she was a widow, with no means of income. She had two children, and her creditors were coming to take them away as slaves.

I've been in nations where parents still face this dilemma: being so deep in poverty they have to give up their own children rather than watch them starve. It's a heartbreaking reality.

In her desperation this widow called on Elisha, the prophet of God. Elisha didn't ask her, "What do you need?" He didn't ask, "How much do you owe?" Instead he said, "Tell me, what do you have in the house?" She answered, "Nothing at all, except a flask of olive oil" (2 Kings 4:2).

That wasn't much, but it was enough for Elisha. He told her, "Borrow as many empty jars as you can from your friends and neighbors. Then go into your house with your sons and shut the door behind you. Pour olive oil from your flask into the jars, setting each one aside when it is filled" (vv. 3–4).

I'm sure she thought, *Well, that won't take long, you crazy prophet!* Yet she did what he said. She sent her kids, and they borrowed pots and pans and jars and cans from everyone they could find. Then they started pouring that little flask of oil. And the oil just kept coming. It filled up container after container, until finally they ran out of things to pour it in, and then it stopped flowing. Elisha said, "Now sell the olive oil and pay your debts, and you and your sons can live on what is left over" (v. 7).

Now, don't miss the nature of the miracle. Only God can take a single flask of oil and turn it into enough for a family of three to live as the Beverly Hillbillies of Israel. However, the miracle did not begin until they identified what they already had. When Elisha asked, "What do you have in the house?" the widow could easily have said, "Nothing." But that wasn't true. She had a jar of oil, and she had empty containers to pour it into.

That's the first promise of the adventure: **you have a gift only you can give.** I'm going to refer to it as your "Life Gift." It's something that is already in your grasp right now, no matter how little you might think you have. When you offer your Life Gift, God will multiply it, stretch it, and make it flow, but the first act of faith is just to see that it is there.

SCARCITY AND ABUNDANCE

God is a giving God, because God always has more than enough. He said, "If I were hungry, I would not tell you, for all the world is mine and everything in it" (Ps. 50:12). Imagine, just for a moment, what the world might look like from God's perspective. God creates something out of nothing, simply by the power of His word. God then gifts this new world with multiplying, life-giving, overflowing energy. The Bible says God blessed the world and said, "Be fruitful and multiply. Fill the earth" (Gen. 1:28).

God started off giving, and He just keeps on giving. The psalmist in Psalm 104:13–14 sang:

> You send rain on the mountains from your
>   heavenly home,
>   and you fill the earth with the fruit of your labor.
> You cause grass to grow for the livestock
>   and plants for people to use.
> You allow them to produce food from the earth.

Jesus taught His followers that God gives to everyone, all the time. "Be children of your Father in heaven; for he makes his sun rise on the evil and on the good, and sends rain on the righteous and on the unrighteous" (Matt. 5:45 NRSV).

On the other hand, our human experience of the world is often conditioned by scarcity. We never feel as though we have enough. We're always scrapping to get what's ours. We tend to see the world as a zero-sum game—in order for me to win, someone else has to lose, and vice versa.

Those of us who live in the United States reside in the most luxurious "subdivision" in the world. As the familiar song reminds us, we have been blessed by God with "spacious skies," "amber waves of grain," and "purple mountain majesties above the fruited plain." Our nation is like one big gated community, protected by fighter jets and battleships. Too often we spend our time fighting over the proverbial corner lot rather than lifting up our eyes to see the tremendous wealth and power we have compared to much of the world. We're envying one another's greener grass while others live in the desert, trying to keep up with the Joneses while many are just trying to survive. I don't say that to be anti-American; I love my country. Rather, I mention it to say that our perspective is sometimes distorted by our affluence. We live in the midst of abundance, yet we constantly think we don't have enough.

I realize that when we're stressed about paying the bills, saving for the kids' college educations, and having enough for retirement, a reminder of "starving children in Africa" can just add a weight of guilt. But what if, just like that widow with the jar of oil, even in the midst of our stress, we've actually got more than we realize? What if our feeling of scarcity is blinding us to how blessed we really are?

During the Holocaust, thousands of Jewish people died of starvation, even those who were not taken by the Nazis to the death camps. Among those who survived, the memory of intense hunger did not go away. Even after they were liberated, some were unable to sleep without a piece of bread under their pillow or on the nightstand. Fear of scarcity drove them even when they were no longer in need.[1]

Most of us will never face hunger that extreme, yet in a way, that is a picture of every human soul: we're unable to rest until we know we have the bread we need. In the prayer Jesus taught us to pray, we say, "Give us this day our daily bread." Interestingly, the word translated "daily" might be better translated "for tomorrow" or "for the day to come." I think that in reply to this prayer, our Father in heaven wants us to understand Him saying, "I've got you taken care of. I'm going to supply all that you need. You can rest and relax and trust in Me."

STARTING FROM ABUNDANCE

Here's why it's important that we start our journey of God's calling in the place of abundance instead of the mind-set of scarcity. My guess is that in the past someone has confronted you with a great need in the world. Children who are starving. Sick people who are dying. Animals that are being mistreated. Students who are not being properly educated. Elderly people who are lonely. Whatever it was, the person who presented the need probably felt passionate about it, so he or she was eager to get you to do something. Take action. Give money. Call your representative. Raise awareness.

Being passionate about meeting a need is a good thing, but I'm willing to bet it didn't feel good to you. Instead, you got defensive. You thought about your bills and your busy schedule and all the demands that already burden you and weigh you down. But you also felt guilty. You wondered, *Am I a bad person? Do I not care enough?* You wanted to help, but you weren't sure you could. And those conflicting emotions just made the whole experience feel uncomfortable and awkward. You wanted to turn the channel, leave the meeting, change the subject.

If that was your reaction, it doesn't mean you are a bad person. It simply means that you were approaching the overwhelming need of the world without a confident sense that you had the abundant resources to match it. You were coming from the place of scarcity. The Land of Not Enough. And in that land, when it comes to going on yet another guilt trip, everybody's response is, *Ain't nobody got time for that.*

So I hope this comes as good news to you: the last thing I want to do is give you one more guilt trip, one more item for your to-do list, one more straw on the camel's back. Rather, I want to offer you a new way to view the world, a different perspective, one that offers you freedom. I want to take you from the Land of Not Enough to the Kingdom of Plenty to Share.

BEING PERFECT

Let's go back and look more closely at the teaching of Jesus. Not long after He taught that bit about God sending the sun and the rain on both the good guys and the bad guys, He gave this instruction: "But you are to be perfect, even as your Father in heaven is perfect" (Matt. 5:48). Taken out of context, that sounds like the biggest guilt trip of all time. "Sure, Jesus, all You're asking is for me to be perfect? No problem, let me get right on that!"

However, the word *perfect* here does not mean mathematical perfection or absolute sinlessness. Rather, it means "mature," "complete," or "full-grown," the way a mature apple tree that is producing fruit is "perfected" compared to an apple seed or a sapling that has not yet reached maturity. Jesus is confronting those who see the world only in terms of trading favors: "If you love only those who love you, what reward is there for that? Even corrupt tax collectors do that much. If you are kind only to your friends, how are you different from anyone else? Even pagans do that" (vv. 46–47).

We see examples of "loving only those who love you" every day: the politician who gives favors to those who contribute to his campaign, the salesperson who befriends her biggest-spending customers, the husband and wife who only show as much affection to each other as they get in return. Normal human behavior is to only invest in the relationships that we think will provide us with some kind of benefit. Jesus said that a cool, calculated way of always measuring "what's in it for me" is a sign of immaturity. It's based on fear and a mind-set of scarcity. It shows we don't yet understand how God's world really works. When we reach the stage of being mature—when we are "perfect" as our heavenly Father is perfect—we will realize how much we have to give, and we won't be so worried about what we get back.

BREAD, FISH, WINE, AND FIVE THOUSAND HUNGRY MOUTHS

Jesus didn't just talk about a new way to see the world—He demonstrated it. Maybe you are familiar with the story in which Jesus asked His disciples to feed five thousand people on a moment's notice (see John 6:1–14). They were shocked and overwhelmed. It would cost two years' average wages to buy that much food, and they had no idea where they would get it even if they had the money. John's gospel says that Jesus was testing them, because He already knew that He intended to feed the people miraculously.

From one point of view that sounds like a divine gotcha game. Who wouldn't fail that test? But in fact, before He ever put them in a position where they were facing an overwhelming need, Jesus had already shown them multiple examples of an abundant supply.

When Jesus first called Peter, John, James, and Andrew to follow Him, they had been fishing all night with no luck. Don't picture a couple of country bumpkins with cane fishing poles and some worms on a hook. These were professional fishermen, trained to haul in nets full of fish to bring to market.

But this particular night had been a bust. Jesus gave them a simple instruction: "Let down your nets for a catch" (Luke 5:4 NRSV). Peter was pretty skeptical, but he decided to give it a try. The result was "they caught so many fish that their nets were beginning to break" (v. 6 NRSV). They had to call a second boat to come over and help them.

And then there was the wedding that Jesus and His follow-ers attended. The bride and groom ran out of wine, which was a major social faux pas (see John 2:1–11). So Jesus's mother asked Him to help out. Jesus instructed the servers to fill six large stone jars with water—more than a hundred gallons. When they poured out the water, it had miraculously been turned into wine. And not just any wine, but the best wine anyone there had ever tasted.

So when it came time for the five thousand to be fed, Jesus was just checking in to see if the disciples had started to get the picture. As it turned out, they couldn't yet grasp what Jesus was teaching. They were not yet "perfect, even as [their] Father in heaven is perfect." But they got a little closer that day. Jesus started by asking them what they already had, which turned out to be not much—just five loaves of bread and two fish from a little boy. To Jesus, though, that was enough to go to work. He blessed the food (remember how God blessed the creation back in Genesis 1), and it multiplied enough to feed everyone. And just to drive home the point, Jesus made sure they had leftovers: enough to fill twelve baskets. God loves to take empty baskets and empty lives and make them full.

NO SILVER OR GOLD

Eventually the disciples did start to get the message. After Jesus was raised from the dead and ascended to the right hand of God, Peter and John went walking one day to the temple. There they met a lame beggar who asked them for money. They could have gotten defensive and resistant, wondering why this guy had to get in their way when they were just trying to go worship God. They could have made excuses for why they didn't have much money, since they had been following Jesus around instead of working their trade. They could have felt guilty for not having a good program in place to feed all the lame people in the world.

Instead, they immediately started thinking about what they already had. So Peter said to the beggar, "I don't have any silver or gold for you. But I'll give you what I have. In the name of Jesus Christ the Nazarene, get up and walk!" (Acts 3:6). Sure enough, the guy's legs got stronger, and pretty soon he was literally jumping up and down and praising God. Which is a whole lot better than a few coins from some guilt-tripped disciples, if you ask me.

Right now you may be thinking, *That's great, but I don't have silver and gold, and I can't make lame people walk, either.* You're still thinking in terms of scarcity. Don't miss the main point. You may not have money. You may not have healing power. But you have something. A cup of oil. A few fish. Whatever it is, that little bit of extra is all God needs to start your journey.

LIFE GIFTS IN ALL SHAPES AND SIZES

The gifts God uses are more than just financial or material resources. Your Life Gift might be a skill you have developed or expert knowledge you have gained. It might be time that is on your hands. It could be the gift of your smile or a few encouraging words. It might simply be the gift of your presence.

Charles Hall is a member of my church who owns an old hunting cabin that was once used as a place for men to get drunk and gamble. But Charles has put it to a different purpose. He brings groups of men to his cabin to experience Christian fellowship. Fathers and sons go there to hunt and fish and bond. In fact, so many men have used the solitude of Charles's cabin to reconnect with God, he has put up a sign calling it "The Healing Place." For Charles, an old drinking-and-gambling cabin was a Life Gift.

Or take Carl Bartlett, a lawyer in our church who specializes in managing multimillion-dollar commercial real estate deals. A few years ago our church had the opportunity to purchase a property next door to us that was an apartment complex. It was a great opportunity, but from a legal perspective our church was in way over its head. Carl volunteered his time, and as a result almost a million dollars has come back into our church for use in mission and ministry. Even lawyers have Life Gifts!

For more than twelve years, Kay Bray served as the volunteer coordinator of our church's English as a Second Language (ESL) ministry. Even in a relatively small city like Montgomery, we have quite a few people who speak limited English. Businesspeople come from Korea to the Hyundai plant, officers come from around the world to study at our Air Force base, and migrant workers find jobs here in agriculture and industry. The surprising thing Kay tells people is that you don't have to speak a foreign language to volunteer. The ESL program is set up so that the instructors simply speak in conversational English, and the students follow along. Kay and her volunteers have made friends with people from over twenty countries—all because they discovered that simply speaking their native language could be a gift to give. English is their Life Gift.

Then there is Alex Henig Jones, a young woman in our congregation. With two small children of her own, Alex felt led by the Lord to volunteer as a surrogate mother. She went through a pregnancy for a couple who were otherwise unable to have a biological child. Alex said her prayer was that the couple would see Christ in her, but she has also seen Christ at work in her life in a whole new way. She had numerous opportunities to share her faith and encourage others who were facing the struggle of infertility. After nine months, she celebrated and shared in the joy of two new parents holding a child who could not have come into the world without her help. Alex's womb became her Life Gift.

Maybe your Life Gift is a million dollars that you don't know what to do with. If so, I'm confident that God can show you how to make a difference in the world with that amount! However, I'm guessing most of us don't have that problem. What your gift is doesn't matter so much as having that spirit that says, "I have no silver or gold, but what I have I give you."

Do you remember the Christmas song "The Little Drummer Boy"? It tells a fictional story, but one that captures the spirit of giving from what you already have. A poor child is invited to come with the wise men to worship the baby Jesus, but he does not think he has anything that can compare with their lavish gifts of gold, frankincense, and myrrh. Then the thought occurs to him: he can play his little drum for Jesus—and he does. "Then he smiled at me," the song concludes, "me and my drum." You don't have to have an expensive gift to come to Jesus. Just play the drum that He has given to you. Play your best, and you will find Him smiling.

TAKING A BLESSING INVENTORY

So how can you discover your Life Gift? How do you find the little bit of extra that you have to share?

A good place to start is to take inventory. As another old song says, "Count your blessings, name them one by one; count your many blessings, see what God has done!" Like the desperate widow, take a look around your house to see what is already on the shelves.

- Check the kitchen and the dining room. Do you like to cook? Is there a spot for someone to enjoy a shared meal at your dining room table? Are there coffee mugs or teacups? Could you share conversations with someone over coffee or tea?
- Check the bedrooms. Are they full? Could God be calling you to adoption or foster care? What about the playroom? Are there toys that need to be played with? Games that could be shared at a VBS or a Boys and Girls Club?

- Check the closets. Do you see blankets or coats that could be keeping someone warm? Maybe you'll find a pair of running shoes, some exercise equipment, or a bag of golf clubs. Could you share that activity with a child as a coach or mentor? Is there a relationship that could be built during a morning run or on the back nine of the local golf course?

- Check the garage. Do you have reliable transportation that you could share with someone who doesn't? Do you have crafting supplies or building tools? How could you use those skills for someone else? Better yet, to whom could you teach those skills?

- Check the backyard. Maybe there's a garden out back. You could share the fruit. You could share the gardening itself.

- Check the walls. Maybe there's artwork you've created hanging there or photos you've taken. Maybe someone has never had another person take the time to sketch their portrait or photograph them.

- Check your calendar. How do you spend your time? What relationships are you investing in? What activities do you look forward to? What are your hobbies, your pastimes, your entertainments? Is there a way you could invite someone new into your life? Or a way you could invest more deeply in someone you already cross paths with?

- Check your work. Maybe you run a huge company with tremendous assets that could be creatively shared. Or maybe you punch the clock at an entry-level job. Could it be that your smile, your concern, your cheerful attitude might make just as much difference to someone today as the multimillion-dollar industry?

You may not see right away what your Life Gift is, and that's okay. Just have your eyes open. When you approach the world with a readiness to hear from God—an openness to the voice of the Holy Spirit—eventually God will speak to you.

A BIGGER ADVENTURE

My only word of caution: don't think of your calling only in terms of "spiritual" gifts. I believe the teaching of the Bible about how every member of the body of Christ has been given a spiritual gift by the Holy Spirit. However, I'm afraid that we sometimes limit our thinking by putting clear lines between what is spiritual and what isn't. We tend to think of our God-given gifts only as those things that might contribute to a church worship service, such as preaching, singing, keeping babies in the nursery, or greeting visitors when they come into the church. As a pastor, I'm keenly aware of how important it is for people to sing and greet and keep babies, but if that's the beginning and end of where we think God can use us, we're missing the point.

The work we do together on Sunday mornings as we encounter God's presence in worship is meant to equip us to carry that presence out into the world all week long. Your Life Gift is just as likely to involve changing oil on Monday morning as it is changing diapers on Sunday morning; just as likely to include sitting in the cancer ward as singing in the choir; just as likely to happen in the local middle school as in a Sunday school. In fact, if you can neatly package up your gift in an hour or two a week, I can safely say that's not your calling. Not that there's anything wrong with a couple hours of volunteerism—I'm just telling you that I'm confident God has a much bigger adventure for your life than that.

HIDDEN GIFTS

Counting your blessings is a great way to start paying attention to what your Life Gift might be. However, gifts sometimes come in disguise. In my experience, there are at least three ways gifts can be hidden: gift pain, gift envy, and gift shame.

Gift Pain

Surprisingly often, a gift may come in the form of past hurts. The pain of one's past can become the medicine of someone else's future.

If you've lived long at all, you have been through some storms, and you've got the scars to show for it. Often we hide those scars away, thinking that they make us less worthy. They deface us and take away our beauty. They show our weakness. Yet to a hurting person, those scars can be exactly the comfort they need. Nothing makes a greater difference in my pain than finding someone else who has gone through the same thing—someone who can say, "I've been there too. I know how tough it is, but I know you can make it, because I did."

That's what the apostle Paul was talking about when he wrote, "God is our merciful Father and the source of all comfort. He comforts us in all our troubles so that we can comfort others. When they are troubled, we will be able to give them the same comfort God has given us" (2 Cor. 1:3–4). God gets us through the storms so that we can get others through the storms. When we come alongside others out of our hurt and our brokenness, we don't come with a prideful spirit. We don't show up with all the answers. We just know how the presence and mercy of God got us through our darkest moments, and we can offer that same mercy and presence to others.

Later in that same letter Paul wrote about a "thorn in his flesh"—some kind of unspecified pain or struggle that he pleaded with God to take away. But instead the Lord said to Paul, "My grace is all you need. My power works best in weakness" (2 Cor. 12:9). God's power is made complete when you don't have what it takes to solve the problem. Paul concluded, "So now I am glad to boast about my weaknesses, so that the power of Christ can work through me" (v. 9). Painful experiences can be one more gift that God can use to make a difference in the lives of others.

The movie *Dolphin Tale* is based on the true story of a marine wildlife center that rescued a maimed dolphin named Winter. Her life is saved by the creation of a prosthetic tail fin that enables her to swim. At the end of the sequel, *Dolphin Tale 2*, the movie creators included real-life scenes of Winter being visited by veterans of war who had lost limbs and children who had either been born without a limb or had to undergo an amputation. It's a scene that will bring tears of joy to your eyes because you can see the look of recognition on each child's face: *Here is someone like me! I'm not the only one!* Winter's gift to them is simply being who she is, injured tail and all. Her presence brings life to others.

In the same way, injured, hurt, and wounded people can inspire others when they allow God to bring His healing power into their hurt. At first, healing a wound may be private, a matter between you and God. In fact, you may spend many years keeping your pain quiet, a matter only known by a few trusted friends and family members. However, at some point the Holy Spirit may whisper, "You are ready to share this journey with someone else in need." That doesn't mean you have all the answers, or even that you are completely healed yourself. It only means that the next step in your journey to wholeness may include helping someone else on his or hers.

It can be frightening to open up about our hurts. We aren't sure how people will respond, and we don't want to be judged—nor do we want to become objects of pity. Sharing our stories can also cause us to relive the pain. On the other hand, keep in mind that turning our pain into a gift doesn't necessarily mean shouting it from the rooftops. It may just mean finding one person who faces a similar challenge and opening up to him or her.

Listen carefully. The Spirit will not push you beyond what you are able to bear, although often you will be challenged beyond your comfort zone. And you can be confident of this: when God calls you to share your pain with others, it is not to cause you more hurt; it is to open up a new pathway to blessing. Paul wrote, "That is why we never give up. Though our bodies are dying, our spirits are being renewed every day. For our present troubles are small and won't last very long. Yet they produce for us a glory that vastly outweighs them and will last forever!" (2 Cor. 4:16–17). It may seem impossible to imagine that something that has hurt you so deeply could ever be a source of joy. But time and time again, that is the testimony of those who allow God to use them in their brokenness.

A few years ago, my coauthor's wife, Emily, determined that she needed a radical change in her health. Specifically, she decided to pursue weight-loss surgery, the kind where a device is used to restrict the volume of the stomach to modify how much one eats. She knew that her eating habits were destroying her long-term health and undermining her emotional wellness. More importantly, she knew those habits were affecting the lives of her children. Along the way, she realized her physical eating was tied to her spiritual health. She sought out a Christian counselor to help her confront the root problems that had caused her to develop unhealthy coping habits in the first place. The surgery was just the first step in a radical spiritual transformation.

For a year, Emily kept the surgery secret from almost everyone in her life. When people complimented her on her weight loss, she simply thanked them but did not discuss the complex issues behind it. She feared that she would be judged by people who didn't understand her motives. However, after that year of walking quietly with the Lord, allowing Him to minister to her inner needs, and drawing strength from His Word, she felt the Holy Spirit prompting her to share her journey publicly. She carefully wrote up her experiences and posted them on her blog. It was a big, scary step. Almost immediately, however, people responded to her post by saying how encouraging her words were as they faced similar battles. Opportunities opened up for her to counsel others who were considering weight-loss surgery. She discussed with them the benefits and the struggles of this difficult process. Even more importantly, she shared the ways she had drawn closer to Christ through her pain. For Emily, an eating struggle turned into a Life Gift.

What are some other ways that hurts can turn into gifts? I've seen victims of abuse become counselors who help others work through their pain. One man whose child was murdered has spent a lifetime building a program for victims of violent crime. He sits with family members during tense parole hearings and advocates for victims' rights in the legislature. A woman who struggled with insecurity and low self-esteem helps younger women learn to find their identity and value in Christ. A young mother whose husband committed suicide helps children memorize Scriptures so that their thinking will transform from hopelessness to life. Teenage girls who grew up in an orphanage go back to that same orphanage to visit younger children and show them they are not alone or forgotten by God. In my own ministry, the pain of a close friend's death helps me understand the griefs and hurts of the many people I pastor.

There is no limit to what God can do when we allow our wounds to be healed by the Holy Spirit and repurposed as a channel for healing.

Gift Shame

The second way that Life Gifts can be hidden is through shame. For instance, I've encountered people who were delivered from addiction to drugs or alcohol. Some have made the decision to reach out to other addicts through recovery ministries. Others have reshaped their lives so that no one would know they used to be addicts—and they want to keep it that way. In order to reach out in ministry to other addicts, they would have to go public about their past, and they're not ready to do that.

Of course, one of the beautiful things about God's forgiveness is that our past failures are erased, remembered against us no more.

> He has removed our sins as far from us
> as the east is from the west. (Ps. 103:12)

This does not mean that we are required to broadcast every shameful failure from our past, or that every former addict is called to be in ministry to other addicts. Your gift may have nothing to do with the past failure that brings you shame.

But consider this: one of the things that makes God's grace so amazing is how He can transform shame into glory. It's a beautiful thing to know that God no longer remembers our sins against us, but it's possibly even more beautiful to see God using what was once shameful as a source of joy, by using you to bring freedom and life to others.

Annie Lobert is the founder of the Christian ministry Hookers for Jesus.[2] You read that right. Annie's calling is to bring God's love and freedom to women who are caught in the web of prostitution. She is effective in part because she herself was once enslaved by the sex industry. After God rescued her, she could have easily decided to stay as far away from that world as possible. It's hard to imagine anything more shameful and embarrassing in our culture than to say publicly, "I was a prostitute." Annie would have been well within her "rights" as a forgiven child of God to never mention those days again. However, she has chosen to see her past as a gift. She is turning her shame into glory—the eternal glory of the precious women she is helping to save from a nightmare life.

Again, your Life Gift may have nothing to do with the failures of your past—just don't rule out the possibility that God may want to transform your shame into glory. Isaiah prophesied:

Instead of shame and dishonor,
    you will enjoy a double share of honor.
You will possess a double portion of prosperity
        in your land,
    and everlasting joy will be yours. (Isa. 61:7)

Perhaps your double portion will come in the form of double gifts—one gift of forgiveness and mercy, and a second gift of ministry to others.

Gift Envy

The third way that Life Gifts can be hidden is through our tendency to envy others. Whether it's your blessings or your hurts, God will show you the gift that only you can give. When it happens, don't be concerned with whether your Life Gift seems as important as someone else's. There are two great mistakes you could make when it comes to your gift. The first is selfishness: missing out on the adventure of giving yourself away because you think life is all about you. If this is you, you may never find your Life Gift because you aren't looking. The second mistake is gift envy. You might think, *If only my story were more dramatic, I could really make a difference for God. If only I had more resources, I could do something that would truly change the world. If only I had more time, more talent, more education, more charisma. If only, if only, if only …*

The problem with gift envy is that we forget that God doesn't need anything from us. The miracle, the transformation, the life-changing power, all of that comes from God. We're just the vessel. It's not how much we have to give; it's how willing we are to be used.

So forget the judgment and condemnation you put on yourself. Forget the comparisons between your gift and someone else's. Forget the "if onlys." So what if your Life Gift is just a little jar of oil, and that's all you've got? Let it flow! Like the widow, you might be surprised by how many containers it can fill. It might make a lame man walk again. It might save some children from slavery. It might feed thousands. It just might take you on the ride of your life.

DISCUSSION QUESTIONS

1. On a scale of 1 to 10, with 1 representing scarcity and 10 representing abundance, which perspective would you say you see the world from most of the time? Explain why you chose your answer.

2. Can you relate to hearing someone talk about a need in the world and feeling guilty, burdened down, defensive, and uncomfortable? Do you think that is how God wants you to feel when confronted with a need?

3. Thinking about the story of the feeding of the five thousand, which reaction do you most identify with, and why?

- Those people should have brought their own lunch instead of expecting a handout.
- It's easy for Jesus to feed hungry people—He's God's Son. It's different for us.
- Guess I better start sharing my lunch; there are still a lot of hungry people in the world.
- Now that we've seen what Jesus can do, let's go find some more opportunities to see His power at work.

4. Read back through the "Blessing Inventory." What room in your mental house stands out to you as a place where you might

have a little something extra to give to others? Are there any rooms you would rather keep locked?

5. Do you believe that your greatest hurts can be turned into gifts? Or does that seem unlikely to you? Try to be honest with your answer. If you don't feel ready to consider your pain as a gift, take some time to ask God if you might need additional healing from your hurt.

6. Are you being hindered from giving your Life Gift by either gift shame or gift envy? What do you think God wants to say to you about the uniqueness of your gift compared to others?

Chapter 3

———

SOMEONE HAS
A NEED ONLY
YOU CAN MEET

Frank and Jan Stevens were an ordinary middle-class couple raising two children. They discovered the adventure of following Jesus later in life and became active members of our church. One of their passions is sports—soccer, in particular. Frank, Jan, and their older son all played in leagues.

After the devastating earthquake of 2010 hit Haiti, the poorest country in the Western Hemisphere, hundreds of families were homeless, living in makeshift tents. So our church got involved in helping to rebuild the island nation. Specifically, we found that deaf people were looked down on in Haitian society, and they were largely left out of relief efforts. By working with a partner organization, we began building a community for the deaf that included housing, clean water, a school, a church, and job-training opportunities. It was an ambitious vision, but we believed God was in it. We called it our "God-sized project."

One summer, Frank and Jan joined a short-term team going to Haiti. They didn't go to build buildings or paint walls or any of those traditional mission trip–type projects. We hired Haitians to do that kind of work so we could improve the local economy and give greater dignity to the Haitian people. Instead, our teams were there simply to build relationships, share the love of God, and work alongside the community that was forging a new identity— no longer as the despised and neglected deaf, but as the gifted and honored deaf.

So Frank and Jan learned a little sign language and set off on their trip. They discovered that, in a poor nation with unreliable electricity, there was one activity that could be counted on to bring the whole community together. It cost almost no money, the old and young could participate, and it didn't require hearing: playing soccer. And just like that, the Stevens family found their Life Gift.

When they returned, Frank and Jan redoubled their efforts to learn sign language, taking classes from professional interpreters. Soon they had friendships with deaf people in our community. This led to organizing "silent socials," a night where deaf and hearing people could enjoy one another. As an added bonus, the hearing sharpened their sign language conversation skills.

Then Frank and Jan headed back to Haiti, this time as trip leaders, organizing a whole week of soccer-related mission work. Using sports, they built rapport with the people, forming relational bridges to effectively share the message of Jesus. They gathered others who had a similar love of sports to go with them. When they headed out on that second mission experience, it was just one activity among many in the Stevenses' lives, a week out of their summer. But while they were in Haiti this time, something began to change. The beautiful Caribbean landscape enthralled them. The joyful way the Haitians worshipped God delighted them. They formed unbreakable bonds with the Haitian deaf community. To put it simply, they fell in love with Haiti. As Jan put it, "When we left, it was just a trip; when we came back, it was a calling."

And what a calling it was. Over the months and years that followed, as they prayed and sought counsel and searched for God's will, the Stevenses decided to move to Haiti. They leased out their house and sold their cars. They partnered with another missions organization and began to raise support. They worked to learn the language. Today their whole family is living and working in Haiti. They head up a major trade project called Haiti Made. Haitians create products with their hands that can be sold competitively in world markets. This gives the Haitians the opportunity to earn a living through dignified work. When the Stevenses are not homeschooling, their children are involved in the ministry right alongside them. And they still all play soccer.

Now, here's the point. If someone had told Frank and Jan, "Haiti is an impoverished nation full of desperate orphans and hopeless adults. You should sell everything you own and move there to help them," what do you think they would have said? What would you say? *Are you crazy?* You see, Frank and Jan didn't respond to a guilt trip. They didn't do what they did because someone made them feel bad for being middle-class Americans while much of the world lives in abject poverty. They didn't even respond to a preacher telling them that Jesus had commanded them to go and make disciples of all nations. Instead, they simply allowed their hearts to be open, and along the way they fell in love with the people and the nation of Haiti. Everything else flowed out of that.

Of course their hearts are broken by the poverty in Haiti. They stay up at night worried about the orphans under their care, wondering how they can help break the cycle of poverty. The needs in a place like Haiti are massive, and that drives missionaries like Frank and Jan to work with great intensity. However, the brokenness and neediness of Haiti is a secondary factor compared to their highest motivation, which is the joyful, creative, overflowing love God has given them for the Haitian people.

When I say the second promise of the adventure is **someone has a need only you can meet**, you may think it is a ploy to pull on your heartstrings and use emotion to try to make you do something you don't want to do. To be frank, many preachers do that, and with good intentions. But I don't believe that is the primary way that God works. God doesn't see the world first of all in terms of need. He sees it in terms of abundance, overflow, joy, and love.

Yes, the heart of God is broken over the sin and darkness and hurt in the world. It was so broken, God gave His only Son to die on a cross to heal that need. As John 3:16 so famously says, "God so loved the world that he gave" (NRSV). God is not overwhelmed by the need of the world, because He knows He has more than enough to give. And He desires for us to see the world in the same way.

SHARING OUR LIVES

When the apostle Paul was traveling around the Roman world, he was beaten up in Philippi for preaching about Jesus. After this, he spent some time with the Thessalonians, recovered from his injuries, and moved on. But he wrote them a letter about his experiences there.

> You yourselves know, dear brothers and sisters, that our visit to you was not a failure. You know how badly we had been treated at Philippi just before we came to you and how much we suffered there. Yet our God gave us the courage to declare his Good News to you boldly, in spite of great opposition. So you can see we were not preaching with any deceit or impure motives or trickery....
>
> As apostles of Christ we certainly had a right to make some demands of you, but instead we were like children among you. Or we were like a mother feeding and caring for her own children. We loved you so much that we shared with you not only God's Good News but our own lives, too. (1 Thess. 2:1–3, 7–8)

Catch that last phrase again: we shared not only the good news, but our own lives. Paul was not motivated by guilt or by a sense of duty or even by the desperate need of the people of

Greece to hear about Jesus. He was motivated by love—love for God and love for people. As a result, he wasn't just checking off a to-do list: gospel preached in Philippi, check; gospel preached in Thessalonica, check. No, he was sharing his whole life with others. Even when following that calling resulted in being beaten or imprisoned (as happened to Paul many times), he didn't give up. If he had been motivated by guilt and a sense of duty, he surely would have quit many times over. At best, he would have carried out his missionary task with a sour, grumpy attitude. Yet over and over, Paul expressed how much joy he received from his work. Joy doesn't come from a guilt trip, it comes from a relationship with God overflowing into relationships with people. Paul continued in his letter:

> Don't you remember, dear brothers and sisters, how hard we worked among you? Night and day we toiled to earn a living so that we would not be a burden to any of you as we preached God's Good News to you. You yourselves are our witnesses—and so is God—that we were devout and honest and faultless toward all of you believers. And you know that we treated each of you as a father treats his own children. We pleaded with you, encouraged you, and urged you to live your lives in a way that God would consider worthy. For he called you to share in his Kingdom and glory. (1 Thess. 2:9–12)

Are you starting to see the picture? Paul worked hard—
very hard. He called it "toil" and it went on "night and day."
That's because while he preached to them about Jesus all day, he
stayed up working a second job at night, making tents to sell
so he could earn a living and not have to ask the people he was
preaching to for an offering. (I know, I know—you are wishing
more preachers like me would take that approach!) However,
the point is not that it's wrong to ask for an offering (see 1
Cor. 9:1–14). Rather, Paul's point is that his love for the people
motivated him far beyond what was technically required of him.
He described it as a mother with a nursing infant, or a loving
father instructing his beloved children. Good parents don't do
stuff for their kids because they have to; they don't even do it
because their children are so needy. They do it because they
enjoy their children, they take delight in them, and they want
to do all they can for them.

That's certainly how it was for Rachael and me when we
started bringing foster children into our home. Just when we
thought we were done with changing diapers and toting car seats
and waking up in the middle of the night with crying babies, it
started all over again. Toil, night and day. But we didn't really
think about the work, because we fell in love with the children,
just as we had when our biological children were small.

Here's how Paul finished up this section of his letter to the
Thessalonians: "After all, what gives us hope and joy, and what
will be our proud reward and crown as we stand before our Lord
Jesus when he returns? It is you! Yes, you are our pride and joy"

(1 Thess. 2:19–20). For Paul, the people God had called him to serve weren't a burden; they were one of his greatest sources of happiness and satisfaction.

NEEDS TO MATCH THE GIFTS

So what about you? How do I know there is a need in this world that only you can meet? In part, because the same God who gives you gifts also creates needs for you to fill. I'm not talking about the evil and brokenness that are in the world; I blame that on human sin, not on God. No, I'm talking about the underlying human needs that exist even apart from sin: our need for food, shelter, companionship, and purpose. Imagine a world in which famine, war, homelessness, violence, and every other evil have been removed. We would still need other people, in the same way that the various parts in a healthy human body need one another. The same God who created the needs also created the resources to meet the needs. Like a lock and a key, they go together.

Have you ever thought about it that way? In certain situations, God gives you a little extra, and He gives someone else a little less, so that there will be a match. By the way, it goes both ways: in some parts of your life, God has given you a little less and given someone else a little more, so that they can meet your need. One student is better at math and another at writing, and they can tutor one another. One worker is better at laying a foundation and another at putting on a roof, and together they can build a better house. Why does God do it that way? Why not just give to everyone the same? Because then we wouldn't learn how to love one another, and we would miss out on the greatest blessing of all.

An old folk story illustrates this idea.[1] In the tale, a man asks the difference between heaven and hell. He is taken first to hell, where he sees people sitting at a banquet table, surrounded by the most delicious food imaginable. However, the only way they can eat is with the spoons provided, and the spoons are so long they cannot hold them and still reach their own mouths. The people struggle forever to feed themselves. They are unable to enjoy the blessings right in front of them. Then the man is taken to heaven, where he sees the same banquet table, the same delicious food, and the same long spoons. The only difference is, in heaven each person is taking the long spoon and feeding the person across the table.

We were designed to be interdependent, each with needs and each with the ability to meet someone else's need—because "heaven" isn't just a matter of having food on the table, it is a matter of having a heart of love that is willing to share. Scripture uses the image of the body to illustrate this:

> The human body has many parts, but the many parts make up one whole body. So it is with the body of Christ....
>
> Our bodies have many parts, and God has put each part just where he wants it.... The eye can never say to the hand, "I don't need you." The head can't say to the feet, "I don't need you." ...

> This makes for harmony among the mem-
> bers, so that all the members care for each other.
> If one part suffers, all the parts suffer with it,
> and if one part is honored, all the parts are glad.
> (1 Cor. 12:12, 18, 21, 25–26)

You see, it's not enough for each part to have something to give. The body must also be arranged so that each part has a need. When the gifts are perfectly matched to the needs, every part of the body learns to love every other part, because they all need one another. God has given you talents, abilities, resources—Life Gifts. And when you discover your Life Gift, your place of abundance where you have something extra, you can count on it that someone needs exactly what you have to offer.

Thomas Merton points out how living for the needs of others helps us accept our own needs:

> It is therefore of supreme importance that we
> consent to live not for ourselves but for others.
> When we do this we will be able first of all to
> face and accept our own limitations. As long as
> we secretly adore ourselves, our own deficiencies
> will remain to torture us with an apparent defile-
> ment. But if we live for others, we will gradually
> discover that no one expects us to be "as gods."
> We will see that we are human, like everyone else,
> that we all have weaknesses and deficiencies, and

that these limitations of ours play a most important part in all our lives. It is because of them that
we need others and others need us. We are not all
weak in the same spots, and so we supplement
and complete one another, each one making up
in himself for the lack in another.[2]

In our church we have a ministry called PAWS, which stands
for "Pets Are Working Saints." It came about through some members in our church who love animals. Their pets are their passion.
Then some of them discovered, "That's my Life Gift: I have an
abundance of pet love, and I can share it with someone else."

However, by itself that discovery couldn't do any good. It had
to be matched with a need. These church members discovered that
animals can make a huge difference in the lives of elderly persons
confined to a nursing home. Contact with a well-trained, loving
pet has enormous psychological and even physical benefits. That's
how the PAWS ministry was born: a furry gift, and someone to
play with it—a Life Gift from God's overflowing love, and someone who needed to receive it.

CIRCLES OF GIVING

Often God causes His gifts to come full circle. Mike and Lisa
Conn are members of our church who both come from broken
homes. They never had solid examples from their parents of how
a husband and wife should interrelate, so they struggled early in

their marriage. Then they got involved in a Bible study class where the teacher gave them biblical principles and practical teaching on how to build a strong Christian marriage. The class was called the Sowers. Mike and Lisa saw their relationship improve dramatically.

At the time, Mike was in the Air Force, and the military relocated them across the country to California. They no longer had their class to attend. In fact, they had difficulty finding a strong church in their new city. That's when they discovered their Life Gift. Someone had invested in their marriage with solid biblical teaching; now it was their opportunity to invest in others. As it happened, Mike's job in the military was being an instructor, so he had plenty of experience as a teacher. They started a new class they called the West Coast Sowers, duplicating the experience that had been so meaningful for them. They built relationships with couples that blossomed into friendships, and they experienced the joy of seeing other marriages flourish the way theirs had.

Today, Mike and Lisa are back in Alabama at our church. Mike is retired from the military, and they lead a ministry called Family Teams for Christ, investing full time in young couples, most of whom are stationed at the Air Force base here. They found their Life Gift, and God showed them the need only they could fill.

GIFTS FIRST

Let's go back and reiterate the order of the promises: Life Gifts come first. Nobody came and told the people who started PAWS, "To be good Christians, you have to go do something for old people in nursing homes." Nobody told the Conns, "You have to start a new Bible study class." They weren't guilted into serving others. They simply found they had a Life Gift. But once they found it, God revealed a need that they could meet, and a relationship of love developed in the process that wouldn't have come about otherwise.

The key word here is "relationship." When I say, "There is a need that only you can fill," I don't mean that you have skills nobody else has. Nobody is irreplaceable from that point of view. Nor is it true that you have resources that only you can give. If you don't give money to some charitable cause, it is certainly possible that someone else will. If we hadn't opened our home to foster children, maybe somebody else would have. God doesn't "need" us in that sense. However, nobody else can form the relationships that you can form. Nobody else can be there for someone else quite like you can.

START AT HOME

Some of us are "people people"—extroverts who love developing many relationships in life. Others are more introverted, preferring to develop just a few close friendships. However, for all of us, whether they are many or few, our relationships are the sources of our greatest joys and of our greatest impact on the world.

That's why scriptural Christianity always starts at home. If you want to follow Jesus, start by loving your wife or husband. If you want to grow in your faith, start by treating your children with kindness. If you are single, start by being a true friend to those closest to you. Remember, there are needs that only you can meet. Only you can be the husband or wife to your spouse, the father or mother to your children, the brother or sister in Christ to your friends. As 1 Timothy 5:8 warns us, "Those who won't care for their relatives, especially those in their own household, have denied the true faith. Such people are worse than unbelievers." We can't really call ourselves followers of Jesus if we don't show Jesus's kind of love to our own family.

However, once you have begun the journey of building those relationships at home, God will very often show you an additional relationship you can bring into your life. Only you can build that relationship. So build it well. As Paul wrote, "For no one can lay any foundation other than the one we already have—Jesus Christ. Anyone who builds on that foundation may use a variety of materials—gold, silver, jewels, wood, hay, or straw" (1 Cor. 3:11–12). He went on to say that the work of those who build with wood, hay, or straw will not survive the fire of testing, but those who build with gold, silver, and jewels will be rewarded when they see their work endure. I don't know about you, but I want my relationships to be fireproof. Let's make sure we're taking time to build them with things that will endure the test of time. How can we do this? The first way is by considering how we spend our time.

RUNNING RAGGED

Building lasting relationships takes time and energy, and we all have a limited supply of those resources. This brings us to another key point: you can't meet every need in the world. God doesn't expect you to do that. In fact, He doesn't even want you to try. When you try to meet every need you come across, you leave yourself no time to build real relationships with the people you are serving. And the end result is that those people become projects. We treat them as objects, like pieces on an assembly line, instead of people.

"Of course I wouldn't try to meet every need in the world—that's crazy," some of you are saying. But others need the reminder because unfortunately many Christians somehow get the idea that this is what God demands. Even if we never put it into words, it can be there in the back of our minds, driving us like a slave master. This week it's starving orphans in Africa; next week it's lonely widows in your community; the following week it's children in the local school who need tutoring—and you're trying to do it all, running yourself ragged.

Maybe a misguided preacher taught you this, or maybe it's just part of your personality. Sometimes we need to have more trust that God has also equipped other people to meet needs. We may think, *If I don't do this, no one else will.* We forget that no one is a lone ranger for God. For example, the prophet Elijah once complained to the Lord that he was the only true prophet left in all of Israel, but God informed him that there were seven thousand faithful followers whom Elijah knew nothing about (see 1 Kings 19:14–18). It's a good thing to take responsibility when you see a need, but if you start to think you are the only one serving God, maybe you need to look around for the other seven thousand.

Other times we think we have to meet every need we see to earn God's love or merit His forgiveness. Let me reassure you right now: God loves you because God chooses to love you, not because you do good deeds for others. The Bible says, "God saved you by his grace when you believed. And you can't take credit for this; it is a gift from God. Salvation is not a reward for the good things we have done, so none of us can boast about it" (Eph. 2:8–9).

GIVE ACCORDING TO WHAT YOU HAVE, NOT WHAT YOU DON'T

"But wait a minute," you say. "Didn't Jesus say, 'Give to anyone who asks,' and 'If someone demands your coat, offer your shirt also' (Luke 6:29–30)? And didn't Jesus also say, 'Whatever you did for one of the least of these brothers and sisters of mine, you did for me' (Matt. 25:40 NIV)?"

Absolutely. But Jesus's purpose is to teach us to have the spirit of giving. He wants us to see how a life of selfishness and greed will ultimately destroy us from the inside out, while a life of overflowing abundance toward others will give life to our hearts. He wants us to get away from the idea of only giving to people who we think deserve our love. He wants us to give freely, the way God gives to us. That does not mean that Jesus has forgotten that we are finite people, with only so many resources to share and only so much time in the day. It doesn't mean God has given up on His plan to make us part of the body of Christ, with our own specific role to play.

The scriptural principle is to give out of our abundance, not our scarcity. Respond from your Life Gift. When Paul wanted the new Christians living in Corinth to take up a special offering for the poor people of Jerusalem, he explained it this way:

> Give in proportion to what you have. Whatever you give is acceptable if you give it eagerly. And give according to what you have, not what you don't have. Of course, I don't mean your giving should make life easy for others and hard for yourselves. I only mean that there should be some equality. Right now you have plenty and can help those who are in need. Later, they will have plenty and can share with you when you need it. In this way, things will be equal. As the Scriptures say,
> "Those who gathered a lot had nothing left over, and those who gathered only a little had enough." (2 Cor. 8:11–15)

In that bit about having gathered a lot or a little, Paul was referring back to the people of Israel in the Old Testament when they wandered in the desert after the exodus. They had no food, but God sent a kind of bread from heaven, called manna. Some scholars believe it tasted a bit like honey graham crackers. Whatever it was, it showed up every morning with the dew on the ground, but it was only enough for one day. You could pick up plenty for your whole family, and no one would ever go hungry. But if you tried to pick up extra so you could store it away like a bad episode of *Hoarders*, it would just spoil overnight. God wanted them to understand that they could depend on Him for daily bread.

In the same way, Paul was teaching that God always gives us enough to share with those whom He has called us to serve. When you come across a need that you can't meet, you don't have to be overwhelmed or feel guilty. If God wants you to meet the need, He'll give you the resources to do it. His real concern is not with how much you give, but how open your heart is to give it. Read verse 12 again: "Give according to what you have, not what you don't have." God is not in the business of driving you into the ground to meet every need in the world. But He is in the business of teaching you how to love by opening up your heart to meet the need that only you can meet, from the gifts that God has freely given to you.

I had to decide both whether I had room in my heart for another child and whether my family had room in our home, our schedule, and our budget. God did not ask us to meet a need we didn't have the resources to supply. He only asked us to be willing to share our Life Gift.

IMPOSED NEEDS

So on a practical level, how can you tell if a need is one you are supposed to meet? Here are a few tips. First, don't let others impose their Life Gift on you. All of us can be guilty of this. We find a ministry that we love and we are called to serve in, and we get so passionate about it we think everyone else should get involved too. There's nothing wrong with sharing your enthusiasm, so long as you stop short of putting judgment on others who decide not to jump on your bandwagon.

Jesus's friend Martha seems to have had a touch of this. When Jesus came to visit her, she immediately got busy in the kitchen preparing a meal. Jesus loved to eat; we know that because we see story after story in the Gospels of Him sharing meals with friends. He even got in trouble with the religious people of His day for "eating with sinners." He would grab a burger with just about anyone, it seems. And apparently Martha had the gifts to serve that need. Maybe she was a gourmet chef. Maybe she had a mama and a grandmama who loved to cook, and they had passed on that skill to her. However it came about, Martha had a Life Gift when it came to preparing food. She loved to do it, and it was a way she could show love to Jesus.

The problem was, her sister Mary didn't act the same way. Mary showed her love by just being there with Jesus, sitting in His presence. To Martha, that seemed lazy. Here's how it went down:

> As Jesus and the disciples continued on their way to Jerusalem, they came to a certain village where a woman named Martha welcomed him into her home. Her sister, Mary, sat at the Lord's feet, listening to what he taught. But Martha was distracted by the big dinner she was preparing.

She came to Jesus and said, "Lord, doesn't it seem unfair to you that my sister just sits here while I do all the work? Tell her to come and help me."

But the Lord said to her, "My dear Martha, you are worried and upset over all these details! There is only one thing worth being concerned about. Mary has discovered it, and it will not be taken away from her." (Luke 10:38–42)

It's important to note that in Jesus's day, sitting at someone's feet could be a way of taking on the role of a student, a disciple learning from the rabbi. Martha's challenge might even have a touch of sexism: Mary was in there with the men, out of her "proper place" in the kitchen. Whatever the case, Jesus would have none of it. In an extraordinary move for that time and culture, Jesus affirmed Mary's aspirations. Mary was more than welcome to be with Him, learn from Him, and absorb His teaching, even though there was a meal to be cooked that they would all enjoy later. Bottom line, Jesus doesn't impose Martha's gifts on Mary, and He doesn't allow Martha to do that to Mary either.

I'm not saying you shouldn't be open to hear what other people have to say about your gifts or that you shouldn't seek counsel about where God might be calling you to serve. God often speaks through other people. But I am saying that if the only reason you feel like you have to meet a need is because someone else pressured you, that's not from God. First of all, you can't serve in *their* gift; you'll be miserable, and you won't do a very good job, either. And secondly, if you get busy trying to fill their calling, your calling is going to go unanswered. There will be needs that go unmet and relationships that never get developed, all because you got caught up in trying to do someone else's job.

Football teams have a phrase for this: stay in your lane. It's easy for a defensive player to see the offense moving the ball down the field and want to rush in to make the tackle. The problem is that the offense can shift directions quickly. If you move out of your assigned spot, you're going to leave a huge opening on the field. Instead, players have to trust one another: "You cover your lane, I'll cover mine, and together we'll make the tackle." When it comes to responding to the needs of the world, Christians sometimes need to learn to stay in their lane.

THE PRIOR RELATIONSHIP TEST

A second test to see if you are called to meet the need is considering how it will affect the God-given relationships you already have. Tragically, the church is full of stories of pastors and church members who got so caught up in serving that they neglected their own families. Some of the most vehement atheists attacking the Christian message today are actually the children of Christian leaders who got left out in the cold because Mom or Dad was always away, always putting someone else's needs before their own family's.

I find it interesting that over and over in the Bible God declares His special concern for widows and orphans.

Father to the fatherless, defender of widows—
this is God, whose dwelling is holy.
(Ps. 68:5)

Because God cares for orphans and widows, He commands us to do the same: "Pure and genuine religion in the sight of God the Father means caring for orphans and widows in their distress and refusing to let the world corrupt you" (James 1:27).

Why these two groups in particular? Because God wants everyone to be a part of a family. The family is God's first plan to care for people. When Plan A falls through, Plan B is for others to reach out to the women and children who have been left without a family and pull them into their own. But Plan B should never get in the way of Plan A. If we get so busy going out to serve the needs of others that we leave our own family uncared for, we're defeating the purpose. We're actually creating more "widows and orphans" instead of helping them.

I'm so thankful for godly mentors who pulled me over early in my ministry and showed me how important it is to block out time for my own family. When you work in the church, there are always needs: one more couple who needs counseling, one more benevolence situation that needs attention, one more mission project to get started, one more ministry team to meet with. It can be so easy to push aside the needs of one's own spouse and children. And whether you have a full-time ministry job or not, it's hard to keep a proper balance between work, family, and ministry. I have to remind myself that my wife and children are not a distraction from God's call on my life—they *are* God's call on my life.

One of my first mentors taught me, "Whenever you have to choose between the church and your family, choose your family, and consequently you will have chosen the church." In other words, when I keep my family strong, ultimately I'm keeping the church strong as well. It doesn't do the church any favors in the long run if her leaders ruin their homes.

One way I have worked on that balance is by consistently volunteering to coach my children's sports teams. Sports are one of the key venues by which I connect with my kids and teach them life lessons. Sometimes people are surprised when they see the pastor out on the field pitching a baseball or directing a soccer team. It takes time, and sometimes it interferes with other priorities in my ministry. But it's worth it, for two reasons.

First, I don't ever want my kids to grow up and feel like God was the reason they were abandoned by their dad. I want to model Jesus to them in person. And second, what would become of my ministry to others if my own family fell apart? It's an illusion to think that we can minister to others in a lasting way when we're not meeting the needs of our own families. We may look good for a while, and people may admire us for how hard we are working for God, but in the end when our families crumble, our credibility will be lost. Of course it is possible that even if I do everything in my power as a dad, my children could still grow up and choose to turn their backs on God. But if they do, it should not be because I abandoned my post with them in the name of "ministry."

PEOPLE, NOT PROJECTS

The third tip for determining the need you are called to meet through your Life Gift is to return to the key word we already discussed: relationship. Remember, God created an imbalance between gifts and needs so that relationships of love would develop. God is love, and His desire for us is to learn to share in His nature by learning to love others. We can't do that in impersonal, transactional situations.

Have you ever been to a retail store that had exactly what you wanted to buy, but the sales staff treated you like you were an object instead of a human being? Their behavior makes you not want to shop there, doesn't it? On the other hand, some salespeople seem to have the gift for making you feel like you are their best friend as soon as you walk in the door. Pretty soon, you find yourself buying something from them even if you don't really need it! There's just something so compelling about someone who recognizes you as an individual and treats you with dignity.

If that is true in the world of business, it ought to be even more true in the realm of sharing God's love. (In fact, the best Christian businesspeople transcend "business" and turn their work into a way to share God's love.) Our ministry should never treat people as objects or problems to be fixed. It must be structured in such a way that real relationships can develop.

I'm grateful to writers like Robert Lupton, author of *Toxic Charity*, and Steve Corbett and Brian Fikkert, authors of *When Helping Hurts*, for pointing out some of the problems we have had in the Christian community. It's possible to meet the needs of people, especially the poor, in such a way that we actually cause harm because we ignore their greater need—to be treated with dignity and respect. It might be a volunteer in a food pantry who treats the people she is serving like parts in a machine, mechanically ladling out the soup without so much as making eye contact. Or the philanthropist who is willing to buy new shoes for every child in the village but could never imagine stooping to help one little girl tie her shoes. Or maybe it's a ministry that hands out Christmas presents to all the children in a neighborhood without stopping to think how it makes their parents feel to have someone else swoop in and be the hero for their children while leaving them out of the loop. What all of these things boil down to is attempting to meet a need without building a real, human relationship at the same time.

FEWER BUT DEEPER

In our industrial world, we have gotten used to the idea that the most important thing is to be efficient—mass-producing items using automated processes. Efficiency is great for making widgets but not for helping people. Pastor Andy Stanley has a helpful saying: do for one what you wish you could do for all.[3] In other words, it's better to build a relationship with one person and go deep than to skimp on the relationship just so you can reach more people.

As I mentioned before, our church is learning this through our mission work in Haiti. It would have been easy to say we were going to focus on the need for new houses after the earthquake and build houses for as many people as possible. However, we couldn't build relationships just by giving people houses. Instead we chose to focus on a particular community: 147 families who had at least one deaf member. By narrowing our efforts, we were able to be more holistic, building not only houses but also water treatment facilities, a school, and a church. More importantly, we built friendships with a handful of those families who emerged as the natural leaders of the community. By pouring our lives into those leaders, we equipped them to begin making decisions for their own growth and improvement. Eventually they didn't need us at all as missionaries—except of course that we will always need one another as brothers and sisters in Christ.

The strategy of focusing on fewer but deeper relationships is founded on confidence in the power of multiplication. Remember, Jesus focused His entire ministry on just twelve people. He preached to thousands, and perhaps hundreds followed Him on a regular basis, but He spent the vast majority of His time with a handful of disciples. Even within the Twelve, there were three with whom He spent extra time: Peter, James, and John. Yet Jesus was confident He could transform the world. The reason was that after He had thoroughly invested in those few followers, He knew they would be ready through the power of the Holy Spirit to go out and do for others what He had done for them. From that small beginning, the city of Jerusalem was reached, then the whole nation of Israel, and soon the entire Roman world. Shallow relationships may have short-term results, but they don't have the multiplying power of deep relationships. Consider Jesus's parable of the sower:

> Listen! A farmer went out to plant some seeds. As he scattered them across his field, some seeds fell on a footpath, and the birds came and ate them. Other seeds fell on shallow soil with underlying rock. The seeds sprouted quickly because the soil was shallow. But the plants soon wilted under the hot sun, and since they didn't have deep roots, they died. Other seeds fell among thorns that grew up and choked out the tender plants. Still other seeds fell on fertile soil, and they produced a crop that was thirty, sixty, and even a hundred times as much as had been planted! Anyone with ears to hear should listen and understand. (Matt. 13:3–9)

It is easy to focus on all the "seeds" that go to waste, all the people who don't respond to the message, all the ones we aren't able to reach. But God sees the harvest. He knows that just one person with deep roots in relationship, carefully nurtured to maturity, can produce far more fruit than if every seed had produced just a small harvest.

For me, what that looks like is knowing that there are hundreds of foster children in our region waiting for homes, but choosing to focus my energy on one or two at a time whom I can bring into my home and love deeply. It's not enough for me to just feed my kids or clothe them or get them an education: I want to meet all their needs. I approach my foster children the same way. I can't meet all the needs in the world. But I can meet some, and I can meet them well.

Every person has a Life Gift, a gift that only he or she can give. There is a need out there that only that person can meet. Meet yours with love.

DISCUSSION QUESTIONS

1. When was the first time you fell in love? What's the craziest thing you ever did, or saw someone else do, for love?

2. Because Paul was motivated by love for God and love for people, he wasn't just checking off a to-do list. What's on your to-do list for God? Who put it there?

3. Which part of the physical body would you pick to represent your part in the body of Christ? Why? What are the strengths and weaknesses of that body part?

4. Review the quote by Thomas Merton: "As long as we secretly adore ourselves, our own deficiencies will remain to torture us with an apparent defilement. But if we live for others, we will gradually discover that no one expects us to be 'as gods.' We will see that we are human, like everyone else." Based on your own experiences, what stands out to you about this statement?

5. Which of these areas is the greatest struggle for you?

- Start at Home: I tend to meet the needs of others but ignore my own family.
- Running Ragged: I need to learn to say no; I'm killing myself trying to meet too many needs.

- Imposed Needs: I need boundaries so that other people don't dictate for me what God is calling me to do.
- People, Not Projects: I tend to focus on the task more than the relationship.
- None of the above: I'm not really responding to other people's needs.

6. Andy Stanley gives the principle "do for one what you wish you could do for all." How is love motivating you to do more for someone right now? What will you do this week to follow through?

Chapter 4

———

JOY IS THE
JOURNEY WHERE
THE GIFT AND THE
NEED COLLIDE

When you first meet Brian and Kathryn Jones, you are likely to be struck by their contrasts: Kathryn, a preschool teacher for children with special needs, is bubbly, extroverted, and jovial, while Brian, a quality control engineer, is quiet, introverted, and unassuming. You'll soon learn, however, that they have a deep love for one another. High school sweethearts, their supportive, kind, and encouraging attitudes toward one another might be almost irritatingly sweet if they weren't so authentically sincere! The other thing you would notice if you spent any time around the Joneses is how wonderful they are with children. Brian's careful manner and Kathryn's love for fun combine to create the perfect balance of protective nurturing and creative enrichment. So you might be surprised that the couple always felt that it was not God's will for them to have children.

But the wisdom of God's plan began to unfold for them a few years ago when a group of girls from Moldova came to our church.

This formerly Communist Eastern European nation is, sadly, one of the centers of the world for sex trafficking. Orphaned girls grow up with little love or support and are forced out of the state-run orphanages when they turn eighteen. On the streets they become easy prey for slave traders, who lure them away with promises of jobs. These girls had grown up in one such orphanage, but the trajectory of their lives changed when missionaries shared the love of God with them and provided a home they could go to when they aged out of the orphanage.

When Brian and Kathryn heard them speak, right away they knew they wanted to be involved. Like the Stevenses, they started off with a couple of short summer trips to Moldova to work in the orphanages. They organized gift drives to send Christmas presents to the Moldovan children. Eventually, they sold their home and moved overseas to work full time with the children of the orphanages and the young women of Moldova.

Now that I've told two stories about couples who left their homes and moved to foreign countries, you might get the impression that the journey of Life Gifts is all about foreign missions. But it wouldn't have mattered whether the Joneses or the Stevenses had found their places to serve around the world or around the corner in their neighborhoods. The point is that they found almost inexpressible joy as a result of what God did in their lives. Hardly a day goes by without Kathryn or Brian posting something on Facebook about how meaningful their work in Moldova is to them, how much love they have for the children they work with, or how much fun they are having laughing and playing and learning and teaching. Not that they weren't happy before, and not that they don't have bad days, but it is clear that God has exponentially multiplied their joy because they opened their hearts to His calling and purpose.

Let's review how we have seen God work. In the first promise, you have a gift only you can give, which comes out of the surplus of what God has already given you. Brian and Kathryn had a surplus of gifts, time, personality, marriage stability—everything needed to make room for a child or, in this case, lots of children. Second promise: there is a need that only you can meet, through your unique relationships. Brian and Kathryn found their need in the desperate situation of orphans in an impoverished country. That leads to the third promise: joy is the journey where the gift and the need collide. Brian and Kathryn didn't just have one or two or ten kids; they have become spiritual parents to dozens of children. And in the everyday journey, the ups and downs and the adventures of doing life together, they are unlocking tremendous depths of joy, like a fountain flowing right out of their innermost souls.

That's what God wants for all of us. As Frederick Buechner put it, "The place God calls you to is the place where your deep gladness and the world's deep hunger meet."[1]

LIVING WATER

Jesus met a woman one day who had an empty bucket, much like the bucket that started my foster care journey. Jesus was walking through Samaria, which was the wrong side of the tracks for a Jew in those days. Jews and Samaritans didn't get along—mainly because the Jews called the Samaritans dirty half-breeds who didn't worship God correctly and didn't have any part in the true people of God. Somehow the Samaritans didn't like that. To be fair, the Samaritans did have their faults; these stories always have two sides. But anyway, the one thing you could count on Jews and Samaritans agreeing on was that they hated each other.

Into the middle of that history came Jesus, tired and thirsty from a long day's journey on foot. So He sat down by a well, and that's when the woman with the bucket showed up. A perfect opportunity for Jesus to get a drink. Only He was a Jew, and she was a Samaritan, and this was not an integrated water fountain. Not to mention He was a man, and she was a woman, and in that part of the world at that time, it was frowned upon for strangers to have conversations with the opposite sex in public.

So all things considered, the woman was pretty shocked when Jesus asked her to pour Him up a drink of water. "What's up with that?" she asked (that's my loose translation)—to which Jesus enigmatically replied, "If you only knew the gift God has for you and who you are speaking to, you would ask me, and I would give you living water" (John 4:10).

Living water? What's that? Jesus said those who drank it would "never thirst again." That sounded good, especially if you were the one who had to walk back and forth to the well every day. But she was still not sure.

A conversation over water quickly turned into a dialogue about religion, until Jesus brought it to a screeching halt when He said, "Go get your husband." Well, that was a sore spot because she had had five husbands, and the man she was living with now she wasn't married to. In fact, that may have been why she had shown up all alone in the heat of the day to get water, instead of in the cool of the early morning with all the other women; perhaps she was shunned by them as unworthy. So she just said, "I don't have a husband," to which Jesus said in effect, "You can say that again," and He spilled the beans. Somehow He already knew her whole story, the good, the bad, and the ugly. But the offer still stood: Living water. Never thirsting again.

So this is where things got interesting. She ran back into the town and started telling everybody, "Come and see a man who told me everything I ever did! Could he possibly be the Messiah?" (John 4:29). Pretty soon, everyone was coming to find out more about Jesus. He stayed around town for a couple of days, and John recorded, "Many Samaritans from the village believed in Jesus because the woman had said, 'He told me everything I ever did!'" (v. 39). By the time He left, they were all telling her, "We know that he is indeed the Savior of the world" (v. 42).

Jesus had told the woman that His kind of water is like a spring inside your heart, welling up to eternal life. And sure enough, her simple act of faith in thinking He might be the Christ bubbled over to bring eternal life not only to her, but to everyone around her. Jesus started off by asking for her to give Him her literal empty bucket, but it turned out that the woman herself was the empty bucket that carried the life-giving message of Christ to her whole town.

Can you imagine the joy she must have felt, to go from being the town outcast, the woman with the scarlet letter, to being the one through whom salvation came to the whole village? Before, anyone looking at her would have thought she had nothing to offer. But it turned out that with Jesus, even the darkest chapters of her story could be redeemed. And with that bucket she brought water to the needs of her city's people, the need for a real relationship with God that could only come through Jesus Christ.

Perhaps all along she had been thinking that joy would come when she finally found just the right husband, but that dream had to have been shattered long before the day she met Jesus. After meeting Jesus, she found a new dream.

Joy comes when your gift meets the world's need—even when all you've got to give are your own broken pieces.

THE THRILL SEEKER

That has certainly been my story. All through my teenage and college years, I thought joy would come through excitement. I was a thrill seeker, a party animal. I turned my back on God and laughed at anyone foolish enough to believe in such outdated and restrictive ideas. But none of those things brought me joy. It was always just out of reach. Until the day the grace of God began to wake something up in me, a seed planted by my grandmother and nurtured by friends who showed me the unconditional love of God.

Eventually I woke up to discover that following Jesus wasn't a boring burden that put a drag on the party. On the contrary, the journey of faith was the real adventure of life, the most thrilling, risky, challenging path of all. Before I knew it, I wasn't just walking with Jesus, I was answering a call to preach for Him. My life has become an empty bucket offered up to Him, available to carry the same grace and love that was shown to me out to the world. Every week I get to see people come alive in Christ as the pieces start to fall into place. They find joy at the foot of the cross, and I get to share in it with them. I get to stand in the pulpit and say, "Come see the man who knew everything I ever did, but He offered me life anyway, and His water became a spring of life in me."

So here are six paths to experiencing more joy in your journey: connection, boredom, frustration, weakness, failure, and multiplication. These are the relational contexts in which we can discover our gifts, meet needs, and experience the joy of God's love flowing through us. We'll unpack them one by one.

CONNECTION: JOY IN THE BODY

If you're not already connected to a local church family, then the first path to greater joy is to make an effort to find your place in one. Or if your experience of church is only that you slip into a worship service on Sunday morning, sit in your pew, and slide back out at the end of the service, then it's time to make a meaningful connection. Join a small group or start a new one, a place where you don't just go to church but where you get to *be* the church for one another in authentic relationships. Why? Because the church is the "body of Christ," and it's within the context of that body that your gifts will have an opportunity to surface and connect with the needs of others, and vice versa.

A church is supposed to be a worshipping community on a mission. Worship is vital, because that's where we give ourselves to God and receive His gifts of the Spirit and the Word. However, community is just as much a part of the definition of church. The church ought to be the most authentic human connection in the world. Jesus said, "For where two or three gather together as my followers, I am there among them" (Matt. 18:20). I find Jesus in you, and you find Jesus in me. The bread and wine we eat and drink in Communion are a participation in the body and blood of Jesus given to us, but they are also a witness to the unity we share with our brothers and sisters in Christ; just as we share one loaf and one cup, so we are one with one another.

Does that sound too mystical? In reality, nothing could be more practical. People in churches are real people, with all the flaws and foibles and dirt and smell of anyone else in the world. We screw up, we hurt each other, we let one another down. But when we're open to it, something else can happen in the midst of all that brokenness. We can encourage one another. We can carry one another's burdens. We can lift one another up in prayer, even when we don't know the words to say. We can become the embodiment of God's presence to one another.

As Donald Whitney wrote, "Anyone who measures progress in Christlikeness only in terms of growth in his or her fellowship with God takes an incomplete measurement. Spiritual maturity also includes growth in fellowship with the children of God."[2] If you have a religion that's just "Jesus and me" and doesn't involve real relationships within a community of faith, you're missing out on the joy God wants you to experience.

> ### Bottom Line
>
> *Active engagement in a faith community creates the relational context where you can discover your gifts, connect to others' needs, and experience the joy of God's adventure.*

BOREDOM: A WAKE-UP CALL TO JOY

The second path to greater joy is to pay attention to boredom in your life, especially when it is new. What I mean is this: Sometimes you are going along and everything is fine; your work seems meaningful, your relationships are fulfilling, you are growing in your relationship with God, and you are offering something to the world. Life is good. Then out of nowhere, a dullness starts to creep over you. Things that used to excite you start to feel old. You feel restless. Or you start to become irritated with things that didn't used to bother you. When this happens, it's easy to assume there's something wrong with you.

However, sometimes what's happening is that God is preparing your heart for something new. There may not be anything wrong with what you are doing, but God just wants you to do something new, so He starts by cutting a few strings that might emotionally tie you down to where you're at. As you open up your heart, fully surrendered to His will, God can begin to give you new dreams. He may be showing you another Life Gift, something you have an abundance of to give that you didn't even realize you had. He may be showing you a new need to meet or a new vision for how to meet that need.

> ### Bottom Line
>
> *Boredom can be a signal that God is preparing you to discover a new calling and is opening the door to new experiences of joy.*

FRUSTRATION: THE ITCH TO DO MORE

The third path to greater joy is the path of frustration. Sometimes when we get irritated it's a sign of spiritual immaturity; we just need to learn to be more patient. However, irritation in certain situations can also be like an itch that the Holy Spirit desires for us to scratch. For example, many times I see young Christians who are eager to learn all they can about the Bible. They love anyone who can teach them, drinking up Bible studies like cold water on a hot day.

After a while, though, I see a shift in their attitude. The more they learn, the more critical they become of their teachers. They nitpick lessons or start debates over obscure doctrines. Again, it could be that they are just immature and need to show more love. But often their irritation with their teachers is actually a sign from God—as though He took out a billboard on their street that says in giant letters: *It's time for you to stop being the learner and start being the teacher. It's time for you to start giving back!*

So what is it that irritates you about your church? They don't do enough for the poor? They don't care about missions in other parts of the world? They don't dig deeply enough into the Bible? They don't have the right programs for children or students? They don't offer answers to the questions non-Christians are asking? What if your irritation is God telling you to go do something about it?

If you have a passion for a particular area of ministry, and no one else is doing it, that's a pretty good clue that it may be the need that God intends for you to fill. You can rage at the itch, or you can start scratching it. You can keep complaining and pointing the finger at other people, or you can open your eyes and see that God's finger is actually pointed at you. Let your response be that of the prophet Isaiah before God: "Here I am. Send me" (Isa. 6:8).

Bottom Line

Frustration with others can be a signal that you have a gift to offer that will meet their needs; your irritations can be signposts pointing to new sources of joy.

WEAKNESS: A BRIDGE TO RELATIONSHIPS

The fourth path to greater joy in your life is to serve from your strengths but meet others in your weakness. You have certain personality traits that make you strong in one area and weak in another. Let's say that you're an extrovert, and you love to meet new people, but you're so busy talking that you sometimes neglect to take care of the details of the job. So, serve from your strengths. Look for ways to serve that will maximize your people skills and minimize your time spent on detail work. Or maybe you're the other way around: you love building a perfect spreadsheet but get stressed out around large groups. If that's you, just because your pastor says, "We need more volunteers at the church to greet new people," don't say yes! Serve in a way that fits your strengths.

Here's how Peter said it:

> God has given each of you a gift from his great variety of spiritual gifts. Use them well to serve one another. Do you have the gift of speaking? Then speak as though God himself were speaking through you. Do you have the gift of helping others? Do it with all the strength and energy that God supplies. Then everything you do will bring glory to God through Jesus Christ. All glory and power to him forever and ever! Amen. (1 Pet. 4:10–11)

Don't put yourself in a position to fail. That's what I mean by serve from your strengths.

However, when it comes to *whom* we minister to instead of *how* we minister, the opposite is true. We tend to want to come from a place of strength. We think, *I've done really well with money, so God can use me to help people with poor money management habits.* Or, *I've always had a great marriage, so God can use me to help people who are having marriage problems.* Maybe. Perhaps. I'm not saying God can't do that. But here's what I've seen: God loves to take people who have messed up, fix them up, and then use them to be the very ones who carry the good news to other people. In other words, relate from your weakness.

Why does God love to use our weaknesses? A few reasons. First, we're less likely to become prideful when we ourselves have struggled in a certain area. It means we're more likely to show empathy and less likely to come across as condescending or judgmental. Second, others gain hope when they see that God has rescued someone who has had the same problems they are having. Satan loves to make people feel like they are the only ones who have a certain problem, so that they will hide out in their shame and never seek help. However, when people see your past struggles and difficulties, it gives them confidence to speak up and say, "I have that problem too, and I need help." Finally, and most importantly, God gets the glory when He works through the weak and the broken, because then the whole world knows that the strength came from Him.

Listen to what Paul wrote to the Corinthians about whom God uses:

> This foolish plan of God is wiser than the wisest of human plans, and God's weakness is stronger than the greatest of human strength.
>
> Remember, dear brothers and sisters, that few of you were wise in the world's eyes or powerful or wealthy when God called you. Instead, God chose things the world considers foolish in order to shame those who think they are wise. And he chose things that are powerless to shame those who are powerful. God chose things despised by the world, things counted as nothing at all, and used them to bring to nothing what the world considers important. As a result, no one can ever boast in the presence of God. (1 Cor. 1:25–29)

Of course, the hard part about this is that it requires us to be transparent and authentic. We have to own up to our broken places. We have to be vulnerable enough to show our scars to others. It's a risk, and I won't lie: you can get burned. Some people may react poorly, judge you, and think less of you when they find out your weaknesses. But that's because of their own inner struggles and insecurities. Be faithful to what God has called you to do. Because here's the thing: I promise there is no greater joy than when you have a chance to turn your scars into someone else's healing. It's such a beautiful, sacred thing when your greatest struggles become the very fountain of love that brings life to someone else.

> ### Bottom Line
>
> *Both our strengths and our weaknesses can be gifts that we give to others; our strengths meet their needs, but our weaknesses help us build relationships.*

FAILURE: THE DOORWAY TO GREATER MINISTRY

The fifth path to greater joy is failure. That may seem like a contradiction. But just as God loves to show His strength through our weaknesses, He also specializes in turning our failure and brokenness into doorways to greater ministry—which lead to greater joy.

One way that I've experienced this is through the brokenness of my parents' and grandparents' marriages. I was never a foster child, but I think in some ways my heart was prepared for the experience of foster parenting by my experiences with my stepfather and also with my grandmother's second husband (I guess that makes him my stepgrandfather). Neither of these men ever had biological children of their own, but they always loved us like their own children and grandchildren. I don't think they ever considered any other possibility. In the case of my stepgrandfather, Allen, I experienced so much unconditional love from him that my wife and I took his name for our youngest daughter, Caitlyn

Allen. In the case of my stepfather, to this day, I call both him and my biological father "Dad." These men came into my life through painful and broken situations, but nevertheless I thank God that they did. They not only gave me a tremendous inheritance of love, they set a pattern for me of a love that transcends biology, which I am seeking to follow now as a foster dad.

The same is true of my years spent running away from God. It was sin, no doubt about it, and I grieve over my disobedience to my loving Savior. Nevertheless, in God's mercy He uses even my sin to glorify His name. I know that now I am more sensitive to the needs and questions of the atheists, the skeptics, the doubters, and the "sinners" in the crowd than I would be if I hadn't gone through that time in my life.

I'm not saying that one cannot be an effective pastor without first having a period of sinful rebellion. I'm just saying that for me, my particular ministry wouldn't be the same if I couldn't identify with those guys who wander into church because their mom or their girlfriend made them do it, but they don't really believe a word of it. I've been there, and I've had them come up to me afterward and say, "Your message spoke to me the way nobody else has, because I could see that you understand where I'm at."

I'm sure that the most broken moment in Peter's life was when he looked into the eyes of Jesus the moment after he had denied that he knew Him three times. Here was the man who had promised to die beside Jesus completely turning his back on Him. He must have been utterly broken. So imagine what it was like when Jesus rose from the dead and came to Peter. Three times, once for each denial, Jesus asked Peter, "Do you love me?" And three times He told Peter, "Feed my sheep" (see John 21:17).

Who was it that stood up on Pentecost Sunday and led the first great preaching revival for Jesus, where three thousand people got saved? Peter. Who led the early church through a time of intense persecution, even after they beat him and imprisoned him and threatened his life? Peter. Who inspired the church for generations to come by ultimately dying for the cause of Christ, just as he had once promised he would? Peter. Was Peter's denial wrong? Certainly. Did God use that brokenness and transform it for even greater glory? Absolutely.

Recently our church launched a new campus, meeting for worship in a local school. We need a whole team of volunteers to set up every week and transform the school into a place of worship. One man who has stepped up to help lead the team is Cameron Sheffield. Cameron is perfect for the job, but just a short time ago he would never have dreamed he would be leading a ministry in a church. At that time, Cameron was at the end of his rope. Alcohol abuse had nearly destroyed his life. He'd even had suicidal thoughts. He had made up his mind that God did not exist. One Sunday morning, he found himself lying on the couch, and something prompted him to remember growing up in our church as a boy. He looked up the church website and began reading the Scriptures through our online devotionals. God spoke to Cameron's heart that day, and his life began to turn around.

Meanwhile, Brian Pittman was a high school football coach obsessed with winning a championship. Although he attended church, God was never a priority in his life; his priority was winning games. Yet, even after winning a national championship, he was not satisfied. He still felt he had to prove himself. In order to deal with stress, Brian rationalized occasional substance abuse. One day he was pulled over for a traffic violation and was arrested for carrying substances in his vehicle. After that, God spoke to Brian through a sermon, and he began to turn his life around as well.

Cameron and Brian became friends, and their families began attending church together. They became accountability partners through the process of finding sobriety. Brian made Christ and family his priorities rather than football. Cameron's wife joined the church, praising God for how He had worked in their family. His nine-year-old daughter committed her life to Christ.

The two men shared their testimony during our Christmas Eve service the year following their transformation. By being willing to humbly and boldly share their stories, these men have reached others, who have hit rock bottom, with the grace of Jesus Christ.

So what is your broken place? What is your imperfection, your scar, your failure that you are tempted to hide from the world? Don't be so sure that God can't use you in that area. It could turn out that this is exactly the part of your life that God can use the most, if you let Him. It may be hard to imagine now, but that wound could become the source of your greatest joy when you allow Christ to use you to heal the wounds of others.

Isaiah painted this beautiful picture:

> To all who mourn in Israel,
>> he will give a crown of beauty for ashes,
> a joyous blessing instead of mourning,
>> festive praise instead of despair.
> In their righteousness, they will be like great oaks
>> that the LORD has planted for his own glory.
>> (Isa. 61:3)

Bottom Line

Past failure does not exclude you from the joy of God's adventure; on the contrary, God specializes in redeeming our failures with His faithfulness.

MULTIPLICATION: HOW JOY BEARS FRUIT

The last path to greater joy in life is to help others find their joy. My previous boss, Dr. Tim Thompson, has three adult daughters, all of whom got married in the same year. The following year, two of those daughters were expecting—one with twins. Tim could hardly wait to be a granddad. He had loved being a father, but becoming a grandfather is like taking that joy and multiplying it all over again.

That's how we should see our world spiritually. It's an amazing journey just to find your Life Gift and begin sharing with a need that only you can meet. But when you help someone else find their Life Gift, it's like becoming a spiritual grandparent. You not only get the joy of seeing the people they are helping, you also get the joy of seeing them experience the joy—so it's double joy!

Mary Causey is a young woman whose life was transformed when she went from just sitting in a pew to getting connected through a small group and volunteer service. She was a stay-at-home mom, but God began nudging her to reach out to others. She was gifted at meeting new people, forging relationships, and making people feel at home. At the same time, our church had an opening on staff. Mary's Life Gift collided with our need. Mary served for a season as our connections coordinator, helping new members get connected and find their place of service. Today, she has taken another position, but she continues to serve as a volunteer. If you meet Mary, chances are she'll be smiling from ear to ear; she's one of the most joyful people I know. Even in her early thirties, Mary is becoming a spiritual grandparent! Her joy is multiplying because she is not only serving others but is also helping others find their own places of service.

Of all the churches that the apostle Paul helped to start, the one in Philippi had a special place in his heart. The believers there were wealthier than in some of the other cities, but they weren't greedy; they consistently supported Paul financially when others weren't able to. Even when he was in prison, they continued to send gifts to meet his needs. Clearly, the Philippians had found their Life Gift.

Paul was quick to tell them that he didn't love them just for their money. He didn't get overly concerned about money; he trusted God to provide for him. However, he did love the fact that because they supported his ministry, the Philippians got to share in the joy of those who were finding hope in Jesus Christ. And vice versa: Paul got to share in the joy of the Philippians as they grew up in their faith. When he was in prison facing a death sentence, he wrote these words to them:

> Every time I think of you, I give thanks to my God. Whenever I pray, I make my requests for all of you with joy, for you have been my partners in spreading the Good News about Christ from the time you first heard it until now. And I am certain that God, who began the good work within you, will continue his work until it is finally finished on the day when Christ Jesus returns.
>
> So it is right that I should feel as I do about all of you, for you have a special place in my heart. You share with me the special favor of God, both in my imprisonment and in defending and confirming the truth of the Good News. God knows how much I love you and long for you with the tender compassion of Christ Jesus. (Phil. 1:3–8)

Do you sense the joy coming from Paul? This was not a man who was depressed because he was in prison on death row. This was a man who was filled with overflowing joy. And a huge part of that joy came from being a spiritual grandparent. Paul knew that he had invested in their lives to the point that they were able to give to others, so he had the joy of seeing their hearts transformed and also the joy of knowing that they were ministering to others who were in need.

Ultimately, he said they had given meaning and purpose to his whole life, which couldn't be taken away from him even in the face of death:

> Hold firmly to the word of life; then, on the day of Christ's return, I will be proud that I did not run the race in vain and that my work was not useless. But I will rejoice even if I lose my life, pouring it out like a liquid offering to God, just like your faithful service is an offering to God. And I want all of you to share that joy. Yes, you should rejoice, and I will share your joy. (Phil. 2:16–18)

Two of my mentors in ministry have been Dr. Karl Stegall and Dr. John Ed Mathison. Karl was senior pastor for many years at First United Methodist Church in Montgomery, where I served my first appointment as an associate pastor. And John Ed helped to build Frazer UMC, the church where I serve presently, from four hundred members to over eight thousand during his thirty-six years of ministry here. Both men worked hard for a long time, and they certainly would have deserved it if they simply took it easy in retirement. However, for each of them, retirement was just another adventure with God.

John Ed saw that he had time on his hands and wisdom that he could share with others. So, with the encouragement and support of some friends, he launched John Ed Mathison Leadership Ministries. He travels around the country, investing in younger pastors who have strong churches but want them to get even stronger. On top of that, he has joined forces with the Global Church Network, a movement that seeks to train hundreds of pastors and plant thousands of churches so that a billion people can be reached for Christ. In order to do that, John Ed travels to India a couple of times a year to train pastors where the gospel is exploding to new people groups daily.

Karl saw that he had a Life Gift of relationships that he had built with many people who love the church. He also saw that there was a need: young pastors coming into the ministry were burdened down with debt from the high cost of seminary training. So he brought the two together, creating the Stegall Seminary Scholarship Foundation. Karl leveraged his relationships to build an endowment that would provide significant scholarships to young men and women entering the ministry. Karl and the donors who support his foundation are becoming spiritual grandparents by meeting the needs of seminary students, who will in turn minister to thousands of believers in the years to come.

As much as John Ed and Karl accomplished in their ministry before retirement, it could be that their greatest impact in life will come afterward. They could be sitting at the lake fishing, but instead they are investing in the lives of people who will bring hope to some of the darkest corners of the world. Their joy is multiplying.

Bottom Line

If sharing the gifts of your own Life Gift brings joy, helping others find their Life Gift brings multiplied joy.

These, then, are the pathways to joy: connect to authentic relationships, use boredom to motivate new adventures, identify frustration as a signpost to new solutions, serve others from your strengths *and* your weaknesses, expect God to turn failures into doorways, and multiply joy by helping others find their own Life Gifts. Do these things and you'll be on your way to fulfilling the command of Philippians 4:4: "Always be full of joy in the Lord. I say it again—rejoice!"

DISCUSSION QUESTIONS

1. What was the best road trip you ever took? What made the journey fun?

2. Reread the story of Jesus and the woman at the well in John 4:1–42. Put yourself in the life story of this woman. How do you think she was feeling before she met Jesus? How do you think she felt about herself? How do you think her heart had changed by the end of this story? How might she have seen herself differently?

3. What are your greatest sources of joy? How have you experienced joy through investing in the lives of others?

4. Of the six "unexpected paths to joy" discussed, which one have you experienced the most? Which one do you think you need to work on the most?

- Connection—getting close enough to people in church to discover one another's needs
- Boredom—paying attention to lack of fulfillment as a signal to take on a new opportunity
- Frustration—seeing the problems that irritate me as calls to take action
- Weakness—being vulnerable with others so they can be vulnerable with me

- Failure—turning past mistakes into bridges to reach others facing similar problems
- Multiply—mentoring others to find their own gifts for service

Chapter 5

THE JOURNEY THAT
BREAKS YOU WILL
ALSO MAKE YOU

So, let's review the three promises we've covered so far:

1. You have a gift only you can give—an overflow of God's abundance in your life, your Life Gift.
2. Someone has a need only you can meet.
3. Joy is the journey where the gift and the need collide.

Now it is time to unpack the fourth promise of the adventure:

4. The journey will break you ... but it will also make you.

When your gift is fully given, when you have done all in your power to meet the need, you will find that it is still not enough to heal all the pain in the world that you care so much about. That will potentially wreck you. It may ruin you, destroy you, cost you everything, and in a very real sense, it will be the death of you.

The hurt is as certain as the joy. Why? Because offering your Life Gift requires you to open your heart, to make yourself vulnerable in a messy, broken world. Giving your gift to meet the needs you were called to meet creates a deep connection between you and others, a connection that becomes a bridge to joy—but inevitably that same bridge allows in some pain. You will be unable to help some of the people you are trying to reach. Some may even refuse your aid. Bad things will happen to the people you love. The truth is, the more you care, the more you can be hurt.

C. S. Lewis explained beautifully why this pain cannot be avoided if we are to participate in God's loving nature:

> To love at all is to be vulnerable. Love anything and your heart will certainly be wrung and possibly be broken. If you want to make sure of keeping it intact, you must give your heart to no one, not even to an animal. Wrap it carefully round with hobbies and little luxuries; avoid all entanglements; lock it up safe in the casket or coffin of your selfishness. But in that casket— safe, dark, motionless, airless—it will change. It will not be broken; it will become unbreakable, impenetrable, irredeemable. The alternative to tragedy, or at least to the risk of tragedy, is

> damnation. The only place outside Heaven where
> you can be perfectly safe from all the dangers and
> perturbations of love is Hell.[1]

Thus, God invites us into the journey of giving ourselves not only because it is the path to joy, but also because the hurt itself is the path to transformation. Scripture says, "Dear brothers and sisters, when troubles of any kind come your way, consider it an opportunity for great joy. For you know that when your faith is tested, your endurance has a chance to grow. So let it grow, for when your endurance is fully developed, you will be perfect and complete, needing nothing" (James 1:2–4). The pain is the doorway to greater maturity. In the midst of your brokenness, you will begin to discover what life is really all about.

Transformation takes work and, inevitably, pain. The journey with Jesus leads through some pretty dark valleys. But it is oh so worth it. We are, after all, Easter people. We follow a God who died and was buried for three days. But on Sunday morning, He rose again. Many Christians want to see God's power, but they forget that His power is resurrection power, and resurrection is only an option for those who are dead.

When I make the claim that these promises of the adventure are guaranteed to change your life, it isn't a slick sales pitch offering you health, wealth, and prosperity at no cost to you. Rather, I want to provoke you to another way to live your life. I want to point you on a path that involves great cost, but also great rewards. It is the *Via Dolorosa*, the way of suffering, the road to the cross. But on the other side is the empty tomb. On the other side is real life. I've experienced this for myself through the world of foster care.

LETTING GO

I began this book with the story of Timothy, our first foster child. I spoke of how much joy and happiness he brought into our lives. However, you may have guessed from the fact that I called him our *first* foster child that he is no longer with us. Foster care is, by definition, temporary. Which means, at some point, his time with us had to end. As you can imagine, that wasn't easy.

I loved Timothy with all my being. I did not know that was possible. I figured I would be able to say good-bye because I knew all along he was never going to be mine. The social workers had certainly done their best to prepare us for the emotion of eventual separation, but some things can only be grasped by experience. When the time came for him to leave our house, my heart was utterly broken. Just a few days before we moved him out, I wrote these words:

> I have to let him go. I have to let him grow. I never thought the first child to leave our home would be my fourth child. The firstborn is supposed to be the first to leave, but not in our family. In a matter of days we will pack up Timothy's things. We will say prayers. We will give hugs and kisses. We will say good-bye to our "son." For 427 days

we have loved him like our own. I will never forget his smile. I will never forget the way he buried his face into my chest and the nights I rocked him. I will never forget watching my wife swing with him and the walks we took in the neighborhood. I will never forget his first birthday party. I will never forget taking him to Stone Mountain, Disney World, and the Grand Hotel. I will never forget the funny faces, funny noises, and funny moments that my "son" brought into my life. I will never forget his laughter.

For our family, foster care became a cross to bear, mysteriously filled with both joy and sorrow, happiness and heartbreak. We rejoice when a child is reunited with his parents, for that is as it should be. Yet we don't apologize for the tears on our faces. Although our calling is to provide a temporary home in our house, we have learned that this means creating a permanent home in our hearts.

I continue to pray every day for Timothy, that he will know the depth of Jesus's love for him. I pray that he will know God's plan for him to prosper in this life. I pray that he will receive a good education. I pray because that is all that is left for me to do. That just may be God's final lesson from those fourteen months of my life—that prayer is enough when you trust that God is enough. My gift was just a small piece of what it takes to meet the needs of the world, and it was not enough to fill it completely, but it was never intended to be. God wanted me to give my gift as a sign to point me to the greater reality: that He alone is the great gift giver, who will meet every need in the world in due time.

"He will wipe every tear from their eyes, and there will be no more death or sorrow or crying or pain. All these things are gone forever" (Rev. 21:4). He is the judge of the world, who will one day set all things right, heal every hurt, wipe away every tear—including my tears and the tears of the children who have no home.

If this book were intended to sell you on becoming a foster parent, to persuade you to take up some other cause, or to simply to convince you that in general (as Jesus said) "it is more blessed to give than to receive" (Acts 20:35), then I should probably stop with the first three promises. I shouldn't dwell on the fourth, the one about being broken by the journey. I should downplay the hurt and pain of giving our son back, because it doesn't make a very good advertisement.

But I want to be completely honest with you. I'm telling you the *whole* story of my journey and the journeys of others. And here's why: because the heartbreak is what changed me. It turns out, as real as the needs of my foster son were, my own need was just as real—the need to become a new kind of person, to be more filled by the Spirit of Jesus, to be transformed from the inside out. The need to be broken, so that I could be remade.

I'm still learning that this walk with Jesus around the Sea of Galilee is no easy walk. My heart has been stretched and opened in new ways. My love for people has grown. My love for my city and its children has grown. My love for my own family has grown. My love for my wife has grown. God's love is so much bigger than we know.

SPLITTING HEARTS

Rachael will never forget the night we took our second foster son, Reggie, into our home. It started with the call. Once you have been certified as a foster care home, any time DHR shows up on your caller ID, it can make your heart jump. It had been a few months since we had had a child in our home. So we knew what that call meant when it came: here we go again.

It's an odd mixture of emotions. There's the rush of short-term stress: knowing our home will be plunged into the chaos of making room for a new family member, anticipating the late nights and busy days. There's the underlying long-term anxiety: wondering how this will affect our other children, asking ourselves if they are ready. But mostly there is excitement. We signed up for this adventure, and we love it. We can't wait to meet the boy or girl we will have the privilege of pouring our lives and hearts into next.

And beyond all of those emotions for ourselves, there is the awareness of what this means for the child. If he is coming to our home, it means he has been taken out of his own, perhaps the only home he has ever known. All that is familiar is being stripped away. *We* know we are going to love him and care for him and do everything in our power to make him feel safe and secure, but *he* doesn't know that. All he knows is everything is changing.

We had been prepared for all of that by our training and by our experiences in our first foster care placement. But my wife was not prepared for that night. It was late and very dark when the social workers showed up with Reggie. As they opened the door to the backseat, Rachael saw that he was not alone. His two sisters, just four and six years old, were clinging to their brother. We were only set up to take one child. The siblings would have to be split into separate homes. They had lost their home, bedrooms, parents, and now each other, all in one night. Reggie was just a toddler, barely aware of what was happening, but his sisters were old enough to know, and they were crying for him, like a piece of them was being torn right out of their hearts. And when their hearts broke, Rachael's did too.

The pain of that night marked my wife deeply. She had chosen to love, chosen to give her gift, chosen to meet a need, and in doing so, she opened her heart to share in the same pain as those whom she was serving. That's what happens in relationship: we can't love without vulnerability, without taking our guard down. Like a Trojan horse, love allows things that can hurt us to come inside the walls of our defenses.

REDOUBLING OUR EFFORTS

Rachael is a tough woman. She's been through a lot in her own life journey, and she hasn't survived by running and hiding. She's an accountant, trained to run the numbers and face the facts. She doesn't go in for a lot of sentimentality. She finds a way through.

So when that deep pain met her iron will, it didn't make her give up on foster care. It led her to redouble her efforts.

We began to explore how we could find a way to afford a larger home or build one with enough bedrooms so that we could be ready to take in groups of siblings. We knew it would take a lot of work, some financial wrangling, perhaps even a miracle or two to pull off, but Rachael was determined that the next time we had a placement it wouldn't be a tearful separation; it would be a joyful welcoming of brothers and sisters who get to hang onto one another.

I'm not telling you this to impress you with our commitment to foster care. I want you to see the sequence, because in this adventure with God, it's all about the timing. For us, the Life Gift was originally room in our house, in our hearts, and in our lives for one more child. Just one. But now we're committed to finding room for whole groups of children. We're no longer just giving out of our overflow, we're actively seeking more ways to give.

Am I contradicting myself? Did I lure you in by saying God only expects you to give out of your overflow, and only then, after you were hooked, tell you that God actually demands much more? Not at all.

God isn't the one demanding more of us. Rachael and I are the ones demanding more! All God asked was that we be obedient to give the little bit of extra that He had already given to us. But once we did, we got involved in a relationship. Within the context of that relationship, we began to learn just a little bit of God's heart.

We grew and became a little more like Jesus. Joyful obedience led to another dimension of relationship with God and others. In uniting our gifts to the needs of the world, our hearts were broken for that world.

Now our little bit of extra is not enough. We are asking God—dare I say even demanding of God—"Give us more!" Give us more of Your abundance, so that we have more to share, because now that we know the need, there's nothing we wouldn't give to heal the hurts of the ones we've come to love.

THE FORGOTTEN MIDDLE STEP

This next step is so important because it's easy to forget how a sacrificial lifestyle looks different on the inside than it does on the outside. How many of you remember missionaries coming to your church and talking about how they gave up air-conditioning to go live in a village in a third-world nation, or gave up the security of the suburbs to go work in the inner city, or gave up their Saturdays to go visit the local nursing home—and you walked away feeling nothing but guilt?

What a downer. It felt like God would never be satisfied with anything less than sucking all the joy out of your life as a "sacrifice" to prove your obedience to Him. But that was not at all the speakers' intention. From their point of view, their experiences had filled them with joy, and they wanted to share that same joy with you. But from your point of view, it was about as far from joy as you could imagine.

The problem is, they forgot to tell you the middle step. In between responding yes to God and selling everything, they had experienced a relationship. They had fallen in love. So it didn't feel like giving up anything to them. It felt like gaining the world.

In fact, that's what Jesus said the kingdom of God is like:

> The Kingdom of Heaven is like a treasure that a man discovered hidden in a field. In his excitement, he hid it again and sold everything he owned to get enough money to buy the field.
>
> Again, the Kingdom of Heaven is like a merchant on the lookout for choice pearls. When he discovered a pearl of great value, he sold everything he owned and bought it! (Matt. 13:44–46)

Now imagine what that man's actions would have looked like to his friends and family. One day he's going along, quite sane and rational, buying fields and shopping for pearls. The next day, out of the blue, he's selling everything he's got. From the outside, it looks crazy. But that's only because those on the outside don't know about the treasure that's hidden, the pearl of great price. If they only knew, it would seem like the best bargain ever.

Can selling out for God be painful? Absolutely. Opening your heart up to the hurts of the world will utterly break you, because the wounds of this world run unfathomably deep. But when the time comes, you will embrace the pain, not because God demands it, but because your own love for the world demands it.

BROKEN FOR THE ORPHAN

My friend Mark Stuart, former lead singer of the band Audio Adrenaline, knows something about entering into the hurts of the world. As the band grew in popularity, Mark had more opportunities to bring focus to the needs in various parts of the world, including the orphan crisis in the impoverished nation of Haiti, where Mark's parents had served as missionaries. Then the unexpected happened: Mark lost his voice. He developed vocal cord nodules, and today it can be a struggle for him to even speak above a whisper, much less sing.

All of a sudden he found himself with a Life Gift: he had tremendous influence in the Christian world through the contacts he had built in Christian music, and yet because he couldn't sing, he also had time on his hands to do something different with his life. The result was the tremendous growth of the Hands and Feet Project (HAF), a mission to Haitian orphans Mark helps to run (also the ministry that my friends Jan and Frank Stevens, who were mentioned previously, work with). It was a tremendous loss for Mark to lose his voice, but God filled up that place with an even greater joy as he began to invest more time in Haiti.

The problem is, Haiti's problems are so complex, even Mark's resources were overwhelmed. Today HAF houses hundreds of orphans, providing them with a loving circle of care in a Christ-centered, family-like environment. HAF has been recognized by many as the best-run orphan care organization in all of Haiti. But there are an estimated 430,000 orphans in that country. As much as HAF has done, it's just a drop in the bucket of what needs to be done. So HAF finds ways to expand.

Not only are there more orphans to rescue, but as HAF has discovered, life doesn't magically get better for these orphans once they become adults. Haiti has little industry and few job opportunities. Despite having had the best spiritual, emotional, medical, and educational care invested in them, they can face a life in poverty that could result in them being unable to care for their own future children, thus perpetuating the cycle of orphans. So Mark has expanded the work of HAF to include transitional care for eighteen- to twenty-two-year-olds. Most recently they created Haiti Made, a trade initiative designed to provide jobs for orphans. Our church has partnered with HAF to build a Mission Guest Village. This is stage one in a long-term vision to see Haiti develop a viable travel and tourism industry that could lift its people out of poverty and restore their dignity.

But all that has come about not because of a religious duty or a demanding God. It came about because Mark said yes to God to give out of the abundance of talents and gifts he had been given. The rest came because Mark fell in love with the children of Haiti. His heart is broken over the depths of their need, and that brokenness motivates him to expand his circle of influence. God isn't asking Mark to do more and more and more: Mark is asking God to do more and more and more. And God is answering.

THE UNNECESSARY STAFF

Moses discovered how this process works. You can read his story for yourself in the book of Exodus. Doomed to death as a child, God sent someone to rescue him, and not just any someone: he was taken right into the house of Pharaoh. For forty years Moses grew up in the wealth and splendor of the king of the most powerful empire on earth. Moses had plenty of overflow to give from. Then one day, God allowed him to cross paths with a need. Walking out of the palace and visiting his own people, the Hebrew slaves of Egypt, he got to see firsthand the toil and oppression and pain they were under. He watched as a slave driver whipped a man, and something inside Moses snapped. He could no longer sit back and do nothing. He had a gift to give, and a need to give it to, so Moses stepped in.

In his first attempt, Moses did it wrong. He murdered the guard he found whipping that slave, and he had to run for his life. For the next forty years he lived on the back side of nowhere, keeping a low profile in the desert. That's when he ran into the burning bush. God said, "Moses, you've got a calling. I'm sending you to set My people free."

Moses complained that he didn't have anything. Maybe he was still feeling bad about how he had mishandled things the first time around. Maybe he was just scared. But he told God, "Don't send me, I don't have the skills. I can't speak well." And God said, "No problem, I invented speaking, so I can fix that. If it's a big deal, I'll send your brother Aaron with you." But

Moses was still hesitant, so God asked, "What's in your hand?" And Moses said, "A shepherd's staff" (Moses's job was being a shepherd). So God said, "Stretch it out, and I'll send my power through it." Sure enough, God used that staff to perform miracles and to strike the land of Egypt with the ten terrible plagues. Eventually, He used it to part the Red Sea so the people of Israel could walk across on dry land.

Of course God didn't need that staff. It wasn't a magic wand with a feather from a phoenix inside. It was just a stick. The point was, the staff was what was already in Moses's hand. God doesn't need our ability, just our availability. God just needed Moses to say yes to making his staff available. God took it from there.

Moses ended up taking on a huge load of responsibility. He had to find food and water for millions of people in the middle of a desert. He had to settle their disputes (they had lots of disputes) and answer their complaints (they had lots of complaints). But Moses had fallen in love with the people. Their hurts were his hurts.

I know that Moses loved the people because when even God got tired of the people of Israel, Moses didn't. When they had been stubborn and rebellious for about the millionth time, God said, "Step aside, Moses; I'll wipe them all out and start over. I'll make a new nation from you." But Moses's response was shocking: "Don't do it, God; kill me instead. Better me than them." So God changed His mind because of Moses's prayer. Look it up—that's what the Bible says (see Exod. 32:14)!

Well, I have a sneaking suspicion that God knew all along what Moses would say, and He only "changed His mind" relatively speaking. But the point is, the same Moses whom God had to persuade to go on the rescue mission in the first place was now the one begging God to make sure it got carried through. God asked Moses to give Him a stick. Moses asked God to save a nation. Evidently, something had happened deep in the heart of Moses.

FROM SLAVES TO FRIENDS

In fact, that's what's really going on any time God invites you on an adventure to give your life away. The real miracle isn't the change you make in the world. The real miracle is the change it makes in your heart. You begin to take on the character and nature of God. When God's process has done its work, He doesn't have to ask you to do anything, because you have become like Him. You want what God wants, so you ask Him!

Jesus said it this way to His disciples: "If you remain in me and my words remain in you, you may ask for anything you want, and it will be granted!" (John 15:7). Some have distorted these verses to mean, "If you really, really believe it, you can ask for a million dollars and it will come floating down from heaven," as though faith in God were like rubbing a magic genie's lamp. But when Jesus said that God will give you whatever you ask for, it is only for those who "remain" or "abide" or "dwell" or "live" inside God's love. When God's love gets inside of you, you are becoming like

Him. And if you're becoming like God, of course God will give you what you ask for because you're only going to ask for what God would want to do anyway.

As Jesus went on to say in the same conversation, "I no longer call you slaves, because a master doesn't confide in his slaves. Now you are my friends, since I have told you everything the Father told me" (v. 15). A slave obeys without a reason. God doesn't want slaves. To be sure, God wants obedience. When He asks us to move, He expects us to say yes. But that's only the beginning. He wants us to obey so that we can begin the journey of transformation and that, in the end, He can call us friends. Friends don't obey because they have to but because they share the same mind-set, the same love, the same purpose and mission. Obedience becomes joyful. Giving becomes cheerful. "God loves a person who gives cheerfully" (2 Cor. 9:7).

STEPS TO GIVING YOUR LIFE

Jesus explained:

> I have loved you even as the Father has loved me. Remain in my love. When you obey my commandments, you remain in my love, just as I obey my Father's commandments and remain in his love. I have told you these things so that you will be filled with my joy. Yes, your joy will overflow! (John 15:9–11)

Do you see the steps?

1. God loves and gives first.
2. We obey by loving and giving.
3. We experience joy in relationships of love.

Only then, after those steps, does Jesus unfold the pain: "This is my commandment: Love each other in the same way I have loved you. There is no greater love than to lay down one's life for one's friends. You are my friends if you do what I command" (vv. 12–14). Jesus doesn't hide that His path is going to cost you your life. But it won't be because God takes your life away; it will be because your love for others drives you to lay down your life for them.

THE REST OF THE STORY

So what happened with our efforts to move to a larger house that would accommodate sibling sets? Several months into our search, we identified a house that seemed perfect, with a unique floor plan with a suite of extra bedrooms that seemed custom designed for foster care. It even had a pool and plenty of land for children to play on. However, the price seemed out of our range. So we decided to reach out to the owner. We made an offer well below the asking price, with an explanation of what we were attempting to accomplish. That's when the "coincidences" started to come.

First, the owner revealed that the house had indeed been designed as a foster care home. She explained that during the years she had lived there, several people had stopped by and asked for permission to see their old room where they had grown up as a foster child. The owner's reason for selling was also related to foster care: her career was in managing group facilities, and she was downsizing in order to pursue a plan to build a new residential facility where foster children aging out of the system could prepare for adulthood. It seemed that everyone and everything involved in this deal somehow related to foster children.

Nevertheless, our offering price was insufficient for what the seller needed, and since our house had not sold yet, we did not feel ready to raise our offer. She made us an agreement that we would have a forty-eight-hour first right of refusal if a higher offer came in. Six weeks later, a higher offer did indeed come in, and we were notified. Rachael and I talked and prayed late into the night, but we did not have confidence that we could raise our offer without first selling our house. Twenty-four hours into our forty-eight-hour window, we contacted the seller and told her to go ahead and let it go to the other buyer.

The next day I had a phone conversation with a coworker who was familiar with the story and told her it wasn't going to work out. "That's not a good enough end to the story," she protested. "I'm going to pray that God changes something." I told her I appreciated her prayers, but our minds were made up.

That day I was flying up to Canada for a TV interview about my first book. That was certainly unusual for me; I'm hardly a frequent flyer. The flight was out of Montgomery with a connection in Atlanta. I had taken my seat, 14B, and started to get settled in when another passenger asked to slide past me to seat 14A. As I looked up at her, we recognized each other immediately: she was the seller of the house.

Both of our jaws dropped. "What are you doing here?" she asked. I explained my flight to Canada, and she told me she was making her way to a meeting in Boston via Atlanta. It was pure "coincidence" that we would be sitting inches apart for the next hour. "I just have to ask," she said after the initial shock of meeting me, "why aren't you buying my house?" I answered that we still very much wanted to buy it, but that it just didn't seem to make financial sense. "We've always tried to do the safe thing when it comes to money," I summarized. Yet as soon as those words came out of my mouth, I felt convicted. Was the "safe thing" really what God wanted for my life? Was it what I wanted for my life? Was it what I wanted for the dream we had of providing foster care to sibling sets? Yet surely it was too late; we had already released the option to the other buyer. "Well, you've still got six hours left if you change your mind," was the owner's response.

I called my wife. "You'll never guess who's sitting beside me on this flight," I said. When I told her what had happened, she responded simply, "I guess we are buying that house." When we got off the plane in Atlanta, I called my agent and she called hers. Today, we're living in the house. We found a renter for our old house. The extra rooms in our new home are furnished and ready. We're expecting our first sibling set placement any day now. It wasn't the safe choice, but we have a bigger Life Gift to give away. If we had never endured the pain of having our hearts broken over siblings in foster care, we would have never experienced God's miraculous use of "coincidences" to open this new chapter in our lives. I have no doubt that we will face broken hearts again in the future, but I'm also confident that our pain will be the tool God uses to continue to transform us into the likeness of Christ.

AN UNSAFE FAITH

The bottom line is this: Jesus does not offer us a safe faith. He does not promise comfort, happiness, and easy days to those who follow Him. Instead He cries, "If any of you wants to be my follower, you must give up your own way, take up your cross, and follow me" (Mark 8:34). Jesus doesn't say this because He is a demanding taskmaster, intent on proving our obedience by setting horrible chores before us. No, He calls us to give up our lives because He wants to save our lives. He calls us to the pain of the cross because that pain is the pain of love, and love is the nature of God. Jesus knows we cannot enter into the life and joy of God unless we share in the love of God. And so He goes on to say, "If you try to hang on to your life, you will lose it. But if you give up your life for my sake and for the sake of the Good News, you will save it. And what do you benefit if you gain the whole world but lose your own soul? Is anything worth more than your soul?" (vv. 35–37).

That's what Rachael and I have found in the process of giving our lives to Christ through foster parenting: we have broken our hearts, but we have also gained our souls.

I wonder what's on the other side of the cross that Jesus is calling you to take up.

DISCUSSION QUESTIONS

1. Have you ever broken a bone? Or injured yourself in an accident? How did you respond? Did you become more tentative or afraid to get hurt again?

2. Many Christians want to see God's power, but they forget that His power is resurrection power, and resurrection is only an option for those who are dead. Do you think of death to self as an essential part of being a Christian? Why or why not?

3. Have you ever had to watch someone you truly love suffer? How did it change your relationship? How did it change you?

4. Thinking about the story of Moses, where are you in the journey of serving others?

- Still in Egypt, trying to get things done my own way
- In the desert, explaining to God why I'm not up for the task
- Laying down my staff, ready to yield whatever is in my hands for God to use
- Praying for the people I serve because I have fallen in love with them and their hurts are my hurts

5. Are there any areas of your life where God is asking you to serve others? What about areas where you are asking God for the ability to serve even more? Who can you enlist to pray with you and "storm heaven" until God opens even greater doors for ministry?

Chapter 6

THE COMMUNITY
OF THE CALLED

One of the happiest memories in our foster care journey so far was having the opportunity to celebrate our first foster son's one-year-old birthday. We had presents, we had decorations, and we had the "smash cake"—that little piece of cake just for the birthday boy to take and rub all over his face. He was delighted, and I'll never forget that frosting-covered smile!

But the best part of that birthday party was the people we celebrated with. A whole community surrounded our son that day from our church's OneFamily ministry. It's made up of fellow foster parents, adoptive families, couples looking to adopt, couples certified as respite providers (sort of like foster grandparents!), as well as individuals who have committed to support orphan care in some form.

The OneFamily community has been the biggest surprise of our journey. It's like the best kind of fraternity or sorority, a band of brothers and sisters with a common mission that we didn't even know we were joining. We thought we were signing up for a solo flight, but along the way we've made deep bonds with those who share a similar journey. We celebrate together in the good times and pray each other through the tough ones. Rachael participates in a prayer and Bible study group with other foster and adoptive moms, where they encourage one another and help each other apply biblical principles to their life situations. The unique challenges and joys they share give them a spirit of unity and an instant bond. And the wonder of it is, we weren't looking for any of this; it was all an unexpected bonus that came with the package when we decided to open our hearts to foster care. As we respond to God's call on our own lives, we experience new connections to others who are answering God's call. I call this "the community of the called."

COMMON GROUND

In this chapter, I want to share two add-ons to the promises of God's adventure. First, how to connect to the community of the called. And second, how to discover the calling in the communities you are already in—your church, your school, your business, etc.

When we talk about connecting to the community of the called, it brings us back to a principle we discussed in the chapter on need: God always works to meet needs through relationships. In fact, God often creates (or at least allows) needs, shortages, and weaknesses in the world just so that we will have to reach out to one another in relationship. Relationships are that important to God.

So how does that evolve into community? Simply in this way: as you begin to give your Life Gifts to others at the point of their need, you are likely to run into obstacles. It might be problems you don't know how to solve, questions you need answers to, or resources that you don't have. The temptation will be to panic or stress out trying to figure it all out yourself. However, God has a different way. When you find yourself overwhelmed, ask the questions, Who else has faced this challenge? Whom can I reach out to for support?

It takes humility and transparency to approach others and say, "I need help." However, the benefits are twofold. First, you may find someone who has just the answer you need. Learning from someone else's wisdom could save you a lot of heartache. Second, as you share your needs you may discover others who are facing similar problems, and that common ground is fertile soil for new friendships to develop.

For us, that happened when we reached out to find other families who were dealing with the issues of foster care. For Frank and Jan Stevens, it happened when they reached out to someone who could teach them sign language; pretty soon their teachers were also their new best friends. Our needs turned into opportunities to make new connections.

THE WORN-OUT LEADER

For Moses, it happened when his plate got too full as a leader. We find this story in Exodus 18. After he led the Israelites out of Egypt, Moses took on the role of judge, and everyone who had an argument with his neighbor brought the case to Moses to decide. The conflict management was literally taking all of Moses's time, from early in the morning until late at night, and it was wearing him out. One day, Moses's father-in-law, Jethro, came for a visit, and when he saw what was going on he said, "What in the world are you doing? You can't do all this by yourself."

His advice: Find some other leaders to work with. Teach them the law and how to be a good judge. Then let them handle the small cases, and if they hit one that's too big for them, they can pass it on to Moses like a supreme court. Jethro said, "If you follow this advice, and if God commands you to do so, then you will be able to endure the pressures, and all these people will go home in peace" (Exod. 18:23).

In other words, being a lone ranger for a cause may feel heroic, but in the long run it's not good for anyone. Sharing the burden is good for you and good for the needs of the people you are trying to serve.

The interesting thing is, right before this story, in chapter 17, we read of a battle in which Israel was attacked by the Amalekites, an enemy nation. During the fighting, Moses stood with his hands up to pray. The Scripture says, "Whenever Moses held up his hand, Israel prevailed; and whenever he lowered his hand, Amalek prevailed" (Exod. 17:11 NRSV). But Moses's arms got tired after a while, so he had to get his brother Aaron and another man to sit beside him and hold his arms up.

To me, that's a beautiful picture of the community of the called: supporting you in prayer and in practical ways while you try to make a difference in the world for others. The funny thing is, Moses didn't seem to get the message from this experience that he couldn't lead all by himself; it took a visit from his in-laws to point it out.

As you begin to explore God's calling on your life, ask yourself, "Who will be holding my arms up for me when I get tired?" If you don't have at least two people who will pray with you, be there for you, and support you, ask God to show you where you might find a community with whom you can share the burden.

THE ENEMY'S SON

Sometimes community comes from unexpected places. Most of us are familiar with the story of David and Goliath—how Saul, the king of Israel, was too afraid to fight the giant, but David, the young shepherd boy, took him out with a slingshot to the forehead, backed by a confident faith in God's power. What you may not have paid attention to is what happens next between David and Saul's son, Jonathan. We read, "When David had finished speaking to Saul, the soul of Jonathan was bound to the soul of David, and Jonathan loved him as his own soul" (1 Sam. 18:1 NRSV). Jonathan thought so much of David that he "adopted" him as a brother, giving him his own royal robe, sword, and bow. From that time on, Jonathan and David shared what is probably the closest friendship recorded in all the Bible.

What attracted Jonathan to David and led them to form such a deep friendship? They shared a great faith in God, and no doubt Jonathan sensed God's presence with David and their spiritual compatibility. Specifically though, Jonathan and David shared the common ground of having gone into battle courageously against the Philistines. Although his own exploits are overshadowed by David's, Jonathan has his own story of miraculously defeating the armies of the Philistines (see 1 Sam. 14). In other words, Jonathan and David had a similar Life Gift. They both saw the needs of the people of Israel, who had been oppressed and enslaved by the Philistines. They were both willing to use the gifts God had given them to go into battle, even at the risk of their own lives. Their common goal and shared experiences formed a bond of brotherhood that provided them with mutual support.

The remarkable thing about David and Jonathan's friendship is that it endured even when the two should have become enemies. In short: King Saul was disobedient to God, and God's discipline was that the kingship would be taken from Saul's family and given to someone else—who turned out to be David. In other words, David became the chief rival for the throne that would have belonged to Jonathan. Saul hated David and tried for years to hunt him down and kill him. But Jonathan stayed loyal to his friend; at one point, he even sneaked around behind his father's back to help David escape. Even though he knew it would cost him the crown, Jonathan stuck by his friend to the end.

Who knows what kind of new friendships you will make as you begin the journey of answering God's calling? You may find yourself in community with people who come from different ethnic or socioeconomic backgrounds. You may find common cause with people whose political ideals differ from your own. You may link hands with people from different denominations and faith traditions. Part of the beauty of God's calling—and no doubt part of God's secret plan in creating both the gifts and the needs—is that it creates a nurturing place where unexpected relationships can be planted that will bloom in beautiful expressions of love and unity.

I saw this happen with my own children as we engaged in foster care in a racially diverse community. We live in Montgomery, Alabama, "Cradle of the Confederacy" and birthplace of the civil rights movement. Let's just say we have our share of racial tension (as well as a rich history of people of faith seeking to overcome that tension). Entering into the world of foster care put us in the middle of that tension: our first foster son was white, the second black. My children had a chance to literally live out the dream of Martin Luther King Jr. They shared meals and toys and a bedroom with a child of a different race and learned to see him "not for the color of his skin but for the content of his character." All of a sudden, black people weren't "those people over there." Black people were "my brother."

Of course, we didn't sign up for foster care to make a racial statement; we were just trying to love a child. But one of the by-products has been to develop a more diverse community. That has been a blessing for us and, perhaps even more importantly, is shaping our children. Within the community of the called, my children are learning the message of Galatians 3:28–29: "In Christ's family there can be no division into Jew and non-Jew, slave and free, male and female. Among us you are all equal. That is, we are all in a common relationship with Jesus Christ" (THE MESSAGE).

GROUP GIFTS

Taking on the lifestyle of God's adventure not only opens the door to new communities, it can also change how you view the communities you are already in. Whatever groups you are a part of, you can begin to ask the question, What are the Life Gifts we have in common? That is, what extra resources has God blessed our group with that we can share with those in need? What unique corporate gifts do we bring to the world?

For example, think about your workplace. Maybe you manufacture a product or provide a service that you could donate to meet a need in a school or social services agency, or just for a family in need in your community. A newspaper donates copies to a local school for practice reading materials. A car repair shop does a certain number of no-cost repairs for single moms in need. A restaurant partners with a food bank to feed the hungry.

Most corporations these days have some kind of community-giving program, even if it's just for the positive PR. However, remember that Life Gifts aren't just "stuff." They can include your time, your presence, and your unique skills. Maybe you have expertise in graphic design or interior decorating that could be an inspiration to young artists. Maybe you have a strong capacity for organizational leadership that could be shared to mentor young men and women entering the workforce. Remember, the best gifts don't just meet needs, they build relationships. If you can drive a backhoe, you can do tremendous good by using it to help build a new community center. But perhaps you could do even more good by letting a young person ride with you while you do that work, giving him or her an opportunity to develop future skills and passions.

CHICKEN CALLS

We have several Chick-fil-A restaurant operators in our church, and I'm always inspired by how they give back to our community. One way they do that is through "spirit nights." When a need comes to their attention, such as a missionary raising funds to go overseas or a couple raising funds for an adoption, they will designate a certain block of time and then donate a portion of their profits from the receipts of anyone who comes in and mentions that they are there for that spirit night. It's a smart business practice because it drives more traffic to the store, but it's also a way to give back. Moreover, it's a way to give that creates community, because friends end up gathering over a shared meal, celebrating a common cause. That's a win-win.

However, I'm even more deeply impressed with these Chick-fil-A operators' commitments to hire workers with disabilities. I remember one worker in particular who helped to clean the dining room of one local store. She also checked on customers to see if anyone needed refills or anything. I don't know exactly what her challenges were, but what stood out was her incredibly loving, kind demeanor and contagious smile. She always brightened your day when she came across your path.

The opportunity to do meaningful work is a real need for every person. Having a job isn't just a way to pay the bills; it gives dignity and purpose as well. Those Chick-fil-A operators could have decided it wasn't worth their time and effort to take on the challenges of hiring help with mental disabilities. However, it would have been their loss. Everyone was blessed when they took the time to realize that a job cleaning the dining room could be a gift to extend to one of God's children.

CHURCH CALLS

Of course it's not just in our workplaces that we can discover a group Life Gift. Probably the most important group that should be identifying and sharing Life Gifts are our churches, and the small groups of Christians within those churches. Every community of believers should be asking the questions, "How can we serve not only ourselves and our own children, but also the community around us? How can we reach out with the love of Christ beyond our walls?"

Two words of caution, however. The first caution is that the promises of the adventure apply to churches just as they do to individuals. Remember, God acts out of a surplus, not a deficit. He first gives us a little extra and then asks us to share it with others. It's easy in the church to get caught up in a guilt trip. We feel like we are responsible to meet every need in our community. Sometimes the world puts the guilt trip on us: "I thought you called yourselves Christians; why won't you help us with this need?" Other times we put it on ourselves. To be sure, if your church is caught up in a self-seeking, self-centered, country club mind-set that does nothing for the community, that's not a scriptural church. On the other hand, it's okay to admit that you have limited resources, limited time, and limited energy. You are God's people, but you are not God, and you can't solve all the problems in the world. Being discerning about where and how to spend your resources isn't selfish, it's a mark of wisdom, maturity, and love.

That leads to the second promise of the adventure: that God gives needs in order to create relationships. The ultimate goal is not just to meet a need, but to express love, and love can't happen through impersonal transactions. I would challenge every church leader to reevaluate any program in your church that is meeting needs, but doing so in an impersonal way.

One of the big challenges we've taken on in our church is to rethink Christmas gifts. People love to give at Christmas, and none of us likes to think about a child going without during the holidays. Unfortunately, we've sometimes overlooked the negative by-products of our giving. If we show up on someone's doorstep and give gifts to their children, it can produce an incredible amount of shame and dishonor for the parents of that child. And are we really honoring God's way if we cause those children to transfer love and affection to the big rich church instead of helping them to honor their own father and mother?

So after some soul searching and struggle (change is never easy in the church, let's be honest), last year we started using a new model. We called it the Christmas Store. Church members donated gifts or cash, and we purchased items to stock our store. Then we invited low-income parents to come in, and offered them the opportunity to buy gifts at greatly reduced prices that they could afford. We did everything in our power to treat them as honored guests, not charity cases. The result was that moms and dads had the dignified experience of being able to give their own child a gift for Christmas. We're still working out the details, but we think this is a better model in the long run.[1]

MY GIFT, OUR GIFT

The second caution I would share is not to confuse your personal Life Gift with that of the whole congregation. Some projects are intended to be shared by the whole church, but sometimes when God puts a burden on your heart, it's just that: a personal burden. As a pastor, I have to be careful not to confuse my love for foster care with a responsibility of the whole church. Our church has rallied around foster care, adoption, and orphan care in amazing ways through the OneFamily ministry mentioned earlier. However, I never want to imply that Christians who aren't participating in foster care aren't doing God's will.

Someone else may be called to love on the elderly at a local retirement home. Another member of our church may work mentoring men or women. Someone else feels called to reach out to immigrants and foreigners in our community. Another goes to prisons to share the gospel with inmates. Far be it from me to imply that the only way they can follow God's call is through foster care.

The key is to remember that the ultimate goal is not to meet a particular need, but to build relationships of love in such a way that we witness to the love of God and the message of Jesus Christ for the whole world. Here we need to remember the analogy of the body that Paul used:

> Yes, the body has many different parts, not just one part. If the foot says, "I am not a part of the body because I am not a hand," that does not make it any less a part of the body. And if the ear says, "I am not part of the body because I am not an eye," would that make it any less a part of the body? If the whole body were an eye, how would you hear? Or if your whole body were an ear, how would you smell anything?
>
> But our bodies have many parts, and God has put each part just where he wants it. How strange a body would be if it had only one part! Yes, there are many parts, but only one body. (1 Cor. 12:14–20)

So by all means pursue your own personal Life Gift—the body of Christ needs your part. And encourage your church to identify its corporate gifts for those needs that you can and should meet all together as a group. But be careful not to confuse the two. Just because your church doesn't embrace your personal cause, don't judge and condemn them as selfish or unloving. Be willing to accept that others may have their own Life Gift, and that all of our unique gifts together are accomplishing something for the kingdom of God that wouldn't happen if everyone's gifts were just alike.

HOW TO START

If you are feeling led as a church leader or a concerned church member to respond more deeply as a congregation or a small group to God's calling, here is a simple formula for getting started. Gather your key leaders and stakeholders for a brainstorming meeting. Divide the group in half. Have one group do a needs assessment on your community. A simple way to get started is to ask three questions:

1. What are the critical needs in this community?
2. Who is stepping in to meet the needs?
3. What are the gaps—the needs that no one is meeting or that aren't being met adequately?

Remember to think broadly about types of needs—spiritual, financial, housing, health, jobs, education, leadership, recreation, reconciliation, marriage, parenting, etc. Also, think holistically about who is meeting needs—your own church, other churches, government agencies, nonprofit agencies, schools, the business community, etc.

Have the other half of your group brainstorm the strengths of your church, ministry, or small group—what you do well and where you have solid resources, engaged people, strong leadership, a rich heritage, and effective processes. Again, try to think holistically. If your church has a bunch of great dentists, that's a strength, even though you may not have a "dental ministry." We have to be willing to look outside the box.

Next, have the two groups swap topics, and repeat the process. When everyone has had a chance to do a needs assessment and a strengths analysis, put the top five to ten gaps each group discovered up on a chart and the top five to ten strengths on another, and then see what happens. You may just discover that your church has exactly the Life Gift that's needed to meet one of the most critical gap needs of your community.

Of course, there are other more in-depth ways to discover your church's or group's mission, and other books that explore this topic in more detail. This exercise is only a starting point, but I think if you try it, it can make for a good beginning.

I believe that in the church we need to learn to think like the ground crew in the movie *Apollo 13*. Tom Hanks and his crew were up in space when a piece of equipment went bad in one of their modules. In the famous words of Hanks (paraphrasing the real astronaut, Jim Lovell): "Houston, we have a problem." This critical piece of equipment removed carbon dioxide from the air so they could breathe. They had a possible replacement in the other capsule, but it wasn't designed to fit: one was round and the other square.

So the engineers on the ground went and gathered up exact replicas of every piece of equipment that the astronauts had up in orbit. They gave themselves this task: We've got to find a way to make this square peg fit in this round hole using only the items they have on that spaceship. Go!

Amazingly, they figured it out, and the astronauts' lives were saved.

Our churches should be like that. There are needs in our community. There are resources in our church. We might not be able to fix every need, but we can make a difference somewhere if we think creatively. Of course, humanly speaking, you could say it's possible that our church simply doesn't have what it takes to meet the needs in our community. But that kind of thinking leaves God out of the equation. If the One who created the church, and the One who created the community, and the One who prompted your heart to assess the situation are all one and the same God, then don't you think there's a chance you could find a way to make your square peg fit in the round hole using the resources you've already got? In other words, don't you think God may have given you a Life Gift?

Looking back over the two key parts of this chapter—the community of the called and engaging your workplace or church in finding a group gift—we could formulate a fifth promise of the adventure. God uses our gifts to connect us to communities, and He uses our communities to help engage our gifts. Pretty cool, huh? It's like God planned all this out. As Paul wrote, "Thank God for this gift too wonderful for words!" (2 Cor. 9:15).

DISCUSSION QUESTIONS

1. What was your first experience of being part of a team (sports team, musical group, debate team—any group pursuing a common goal together)? How did the relationships you built differ from other kinds of friendships?

2. Why do you think we try to be the "lone ranger for Jesus"? Why do you think God prefers to call us to ministry as part of a team rather than as isolated individuals?

3. Who holds up your arms like the men who supported Moses through the battle? What are some small, practical ways you've been encouraged by others? Whose arms do *you* hold up? What could you do to encourage them this week?

4. Which of these groups could you help to explore ways to serve together? How will you start the conversation?

- The company you work for or the business you own
- Your church or a ministry you volunteer with
- Your school or your children's school
- Your neighborhood or your city
- Your hobby group (golf buddies, bowling league, motorcycle club, etc.)
- Other

Chapter 7

———

MISSED CALLS

Sometimes I wonder, what would life have been like if I had said no to foster care that day on the beach, just as I had been saying no to Rachael for months prior? What if I had hardened my heart, justified my mind with excuses, and moved on to other things? Would God have kept knocking on the door, or would the opportunity have been lost forever? I know there are other callings to which I have said no, and I am sure there are blessings I have missed out on as a result.

At some point, we all lose perspective and begin to question our decisions. We think, *Wouldn't life have been easier if I had just kept the status quo? Why did I have to go and turn my life upside down for God?* Because it is normal for us to get discouraged, I think there is some value in looking at the stories of those who said no to God's adventure. In those moments of doubt, we need to be reminded that, yes, following Jesus brings new problems, but choosing not to follow Jesus has consequences of its own.

RICH BUT SAD

The classic case of saying no to Jesus is the so-called "rich young ruler." In Matthew, Mark, and Luke's gospels we read of how this powerful, wealthy, highly religious young man came to Jesus with a desire to inherit eternal life—to be a part of God's kingdom. Jesus said, in essence, "If you want to live, obey God's law." We know that the young man was a faithful follower of God's law up to that point in his life, because when he said to Jesus, "I've obeyed all these commandments since I was young" (Mark 10:20), Jesus didn't challenge him. (He may not have been as perfect as he thought he was, but Jesus didn't choose to point that out.) Instead Jesus offered him this invitation: "Go and sell all your possessions and give the money to the poor, and you will have treasure in heaven. Then come, follow me" (v. 21).

It's easy to misunderstand what Jesus was saying. He was not setting up a test for eternal life as if to say, "No one can get to heaven unless they sell all their possessions." Rather, He was looking into the heart of this young man and seeing the point of resistance, the barrier between him and God. Jesus knows eternal life isn't really a thing that you can obtain; eternal life is knowing God, the source of all life, and being filled with God's love and free from sin and selfishness. In a word, eternal life is following Jesus.

The Bible is very clear that Jesus was not antagonistic to this young man or his wealth; in fact, we read, "Looking at the man, Jesus felt genuine love for him" (v. 21). Because Jesus loved him so much, He wanted the man to experience real life, and He knew that wouldn't happen until the man let go of the things hindering him from following Jesus.

Unfortunately, the ruler calculated the pros and cons of giving up his wealth versus following Jesus and decided to walk away. The Bible says, "The man's face fell, and he went away sad, for he had many possessions" (v. 22). To which Jesus responded, "How hard it is for the rich to enter the Kingdom of God!" (v. 23). Jesus makes it clear that it's not *impossible* to be rich and follow Him ("Everything is possible with God," He said in verse 27); nevertheless, it's more difficult, because the wealthy tend to trust in their wealth to bring them happiness, joy, meaning, and purpose in life instead of trusting in God, who is the real source of all those things.

Let's put this in terms of your Life Gift. Remember, your Life Gift is the gift that only you can give, the little bit of extra God has already given you that He invites you to share with the world, so that you can become like God, overflowing with love and life. What we learn from the rich young ruler is "the bigger your Life Gift, the sadder you will be if you choose to keep it to yourself." Don't miss that. Having more to give is a good thing; it means you can meet bigger needs. However, having more to give is also a dangerous thing, because there's a proportionately greater risk that your heart will get so wrapped up with what you've already got that you won't want to give it away, and it will end up becoming a trap.

As Paul wrote to Timothy,

> People who long to be rich fall into temptation and are trapped by many foolish and harmful desires that plunge them into ruin and destruction. For the love of money is the root of all kinds of evil. And some people, craving money, have wandered from the true faith and pierced themselves with many sorrows. (1 Tim. 6:9–10)

But Paul didn't just warn about the dangers of riches, he offered a solution:

> Teach those who are rich in this world not to be proud and not to trust in their money, which is so unreliable. Their trust should be in God, who richly gives us all we need for our enjoyment. Tell them to use their money to do good. They should be rich in good works and generous to those in need, always being ready to share with others. By doing this they will be storing up their treasure as a good foundation for the future so that they may experience true life. (vv. 17–19)

In his book *David and Goliath*, journalist Malcolm Gladwell explored the paradoxical curve between poverty and wealth when it comes to training our children. Up to a certain point, he explained, more wealth is an advantage, because it gives us more options and resources to offer our children. However, past a certain point, wealth tends to undermine parenting, because it makes children feel that they don't need to develop the very character qualities that enabled their parents to obtain wealth in the first place.[1] Gladwell's curve reflects the spirit of Proverbs 30:8–9:

> First, help me never to tell a lie.
> Second, give me neither poverty nor riches!
> Give me just enough to satisfy my needs.
> For if I grow rich, I may deny you and say,
> "Who is the LORD?"
> And if I am too poor, I may steal and thus
> insult God's holy name.

However, the ultimate solution is not to strive to be "middle class." The solution is to recognize wealth as a gift, a trust from God for us to give from.

BALANCING THE COSTS

Understanding the potential damage that wealth can do to our children if we're not careful is an important factor in wisely balancing our commitments. Sometimes as a foster parent I had my doubts: Was I shortchanging my other children by taking in another? Were the time, energy, and money being spent on that child detracting from what my son and daughters needed from their mom and dad? It's great in theory to say, "We've got room in our home for one more child," but when your teenage daughter is having an emotional crisis at the same time that the baby's diaper just exploded, there's only so much of you to go around and wipe up the messes. In those moments, you have to make real decisions, and you can easily second-guess your calling.

That's when I had to remember: yes, taking on this child is costing my daughter something. But not taking this road would have cost her something too. It would have cost her missed opportunities, missed potential for growth, missed memories, missed joy. In the long run, I can trust that it is worth it.

This is the flip side of what we saw in the chapter on finding your need. There we said that God will never call you to meet a need in a way that destroys the relationships you already have in your life. I never want my children to feel like I don't have time for them because I'm too busy doing "God stuff." However, I also have to keep in mind the real possibility that they could gain the whole world but lose their souls. No amount of money or time from me could be worth more than helping my children develop a relationship with the living God. Giving to them is part of how I show love to them, but so is helping them learn to sacrifice themselves and give to others.

Balancing the two sides requires wisdom; there is no one-size-fits-all solution. That's why we should never judge someone else's family and say, "They should do more for God's kingdom," or conversely, "They shouldn't try to do so much." Each person must discern for herself what God's calling is. However, in order to discern wisely, we must keep in mind that riches have their own set of costs.

CHURCH RICH

At this point you may be saying, "No danger for me; I'm far from rich." Possibly, but I would remind you that, compared to the rest of the world, pretty much everyone in America is rich. More importantly, there is more than one way to be rich. For example, it's possible to be "church rich."

I didn't grow up going to church regularly. Although my parents are strongly involved in their churches now, they were not particularly devout during my childhood years. I went to church occasionally with my mother, and my grandmother was a tremendous influence on my faith, but Christ was not a big part of my life. In college, I walked away from God completely for a time. It's a testimony to the power of God's grace that Jesus drew me back to Himself and even saw fit to call me into the ministry. At any rate, partly through my own choices and partly through my parents' choices at that time, you might say that I grew up "church poor."

My own children, however, have the opposite experience. As preacher's kids, they are immersed in church life almost 24/7. They go to worship and Sunday school every week, attend VBS, sing in choirs, participate in service projects, and go on mission trips. On top of all that, we do devotions at home, say prayers together as a family, and infuse our Christian values into virtually every conversation. Our children are "church rich."

Don't get me wrong: I wouldn't change a thing about how we are parenting our children when it comes to being involved in the church. We're doing our best to live out the instruction of

Deuteronomy 6:7: "Repeat [God's commands] again and again to your children. Talk about them when you are at home and when you are on the road, when you are going to bed and when you are getting up."

Nevertheless, because our children are church rich, I'm intensely aware of Jesus's words, "When someone has been given much, much will be required in return" (Luke 12:48). Remember the principle from the rich young ruler: the bigger your Life Gift, the sadder you will be if you don't give it away. In my family's case, we've got a big Life Gift. We've been surrounded with many resources for spiritual growth and discipleship. We've got a huge potential to meet needs in the world, which means we've got a huge opportunity to experience the joy of the Lord. We're blessed! However, that blessing will turn into a curse if we choose to keep it to ourselves and not give it away. All of our church activities could potentially turn out to be the thing that hinders us from following Jesus if we aren't willing to "sell it all and give it to the poor," metaphorically speaking.

SPIRITUAL OBESITY

Let me change my analogy from the world of wealth to the world of exercise, because my family is heavily into sports. Football is big in our state, and it's not uncommon to see guys who play on the offensive or defensive line who weigh over three hundred pounds yet are exceptionally athletic. Not only can they bench-press an elephant, they can run faster than a lot of guys half their size. In order to maintain that kind of size and athleticism, they learn to consume an enormous amount of calories. Some players eat more for breakfast the day of a game than the rest of us eat in a week. And it's not a problem, because out on the field they burn those calories and then some.

The problem comes after these guys retire. They are no longer in training, burning up all those calories, but they tend to maintain the same eating habits. The result over time can be debilitating injuries to the knees, hips, back, and other load-bearing parts of the body, not to mention the possible effects on the heart.

The same thing can happen to those who become "spiritual heavyweights." Before we got involved in foster care, I would dare say that my family had become spiritually obese. We were partaking in a continual banquet of Bible study, worship services, and other opportunities to feed our faith. Nothing wrong with that, for as Peter wrote, "Like newborn babies, you must crave pure spiritual milk so that you will grow into a full experience of salvation. Cry out for this nourishment, now that you have had a taste of the Lord's kindness" (1 Pet. 2:2–3).

However, if all we do is eat and never exercise, we start to layer on spiritual fat that drags us down. Pride and self-righteousness can set in; we can start to think we are better than others because of all our spiritual activities. We become complacent and comfortable, and stop listening daily for the voice of Jesus. We forget that we are saved by grace and start to think we deserve God's love because we're somehow special. We lose our first love and replace a living relationship with Jesus with a performance-based game of going through the motions. We're less concerned with loving God and more concerned with looking good to other Christians. I never want that to happen to me or my family!

I believe that's one reason God opened my eyes that day to the calling of foster care. Bringing a needy child into our home became a constant way for our family to match our exercise with our eating. We have constant opportunities to practice what we preach and live out what we are learning. We get daily reps every time we have to show patience with an irritable child, share our toys, change our schedule, and put someone else's interests before our own (see Phil. 2:4). Maybe if we weren't eating so much spiritually, we couldn't handle foster care, but because we are, we would be in trouble if we *didn't* have foster care. Did you get that? We need the need!

That's why I would never want someone to look at me and say, "What a great guy for choosing to be a foster parent." In a very real sense, foster care isn't about me rescuing a child, it's about God rescuing me! He is rescuing me from my own tendencies to become prideful, self-righteous, self-centered, and lazy. Like a great physical trainer, God knows exactly what I need to keep me in shape and prevent injuries to my soul.

FOR SUCH A TIME AS THIS

Let's look at another story from Scripture, only this time more positive: someone who had the opportunity and the temptation to walk away from God's calling, but ultimately chose not to do so. I'm talking about the story of Esther.

Esther didn't start off rich by any means. She was a Jew during the time when the nation of Israel had been defeated and carried away captive into foreign lands—in her case, Persia (modern Iran). What's more, Esther was an orphan. We don't know how her parents died; we only know that she was being raised by her uncle, Mordecai, a wise and godly man.

Esther's story (found in the Old Testament book that bears her name) started to change when the king got a divorce and decided to host an ancient version of *The Bachelor* to find himself a new wife. Long story short, Esther got the rose and ended up Queen of Persia. It's a rags-to-riches, Cinderella kind of story. However, the fairly tale came to a crashing halt when the king's chief advisor, Haman, persuaded him to sign on to a genocidal plan to exterminate the Jews. At this point, the king didn't know that his beautiful new bride was one of the people who would get the ax.

So Mordecai came to Esther and said to her, in essence, "You have a Life Gift." Her gift was not of wealth or resources; it was a gift of influence. She had access to the king. She didn't ask for it or seek it out, but she had it, and now the question was, how would she use it? Because the one downside was, even though she was his wife, according to Persian law if Esther went in to see the king without an invitation, she could be executed on the spot. Apparently the kings of Persia never went to a marriage communication workshop.

In the face of this danger, Mordecai gave Esther a warning. "Don't think for a moment that because you're in the palace you will escape when all other Jews are killed," he said. "If you keep quiet at a time like this, deliverance and relief for the Jews will arise from some other place, but you and your relatives will die." Ouch. That might sound harsh, but remember, Mordecai was one of those relatives. His life was at stake too. But he went on to frame this tough warning in terms of God's perfect timing: "Who knows if perhaps you were made queen for just such a time as this?" (Esther 4:13–14).

Here's the tough-love side of what God is saying to you and me through Esther: don't think that it's just a random coincidence that you have a gift to give at the exact same time the world around you has a need. God planned it that way. He carefully prepared it, and now God expects you to act on it. If you refuse, God's plan will still go forward. His kingdom will still come. He will still find a way to accomplish His purpose in the world, but you will be left out. You'll miss your opportunity. Right now, you may see the costs of giving your Life Gift away, and they may scare you, but don't be fooled: there are also costs of not giving it away, and those costs are far worse in the long run.

The good news is, Esther said yes to God. She went to the king, and he didn't kill her. Not only was she able to persuade him to save the Jews, but God turned it into an opportunity for Haman and all the other enemies of God's people to be soundly defeated. Imagine the joy that Esther had knowing she had been used by God to literally save thousands of lives, including her own. To this day, the Jewish people celebrate a holiday every year, Purim, to remember what God did through Esther.

LOVE THAT KEEPS KNOCKING

I don't want it to sound like God is a bully who demands that you give up everything or suffer the consequences. Remember the third promise of the adventure: joy is the journey where your gift and the world's need collide. The reason God invites us to share our Life Gift is because He loves us so much He wants us to experience the maximum amount of joy possible. And God knows that true joy comes not from what we hang on to, but from what we give away.

Because God wants the very best for us, the Holy Spirit is persistent about knocking on the door of our hearts. Even when we say no to the voice of God initially, He keeps pursuing us. I have no doubt that is why God spoke to me that day at the beach, even after I had said no to my wife repeatedly. My heavenly Father had a gift for me, and He didn't want me to miss out on it. I'm so thankful for that.

So what *would* have happened if I had said no to foster care? I would have missed out, our foster children would have missed out, our marriage would have missed out, and our other children would have missed out on a blessing. Spiritual obesity could have seriously injured our souls. However, I'm also confident that God would have once again knocked on the door of our hearts. He would have issued another invitation to join Him on the amazing journey of joy. As long as I was breathing, God would not have given up on me.

I tell you that so you will know: even if you have missed a calling from God in the past, it's not too late for you. "With God everything is possible" (Matt. 19:26). He has a bright future for you. "I correct and discipline everyone I love. So be diligent and turn from your indifference," said Jesus. "Look! I stand at the door and knock. If you hear my voice and open the door, I will come in, and we will share a meal together as friends" (Rev. 3:19–20).

Let's open the door and join the adventure.

DISCUSSION QUESTIONS

1. Have you ever missed an important call on your phone? How did it happen, and what were the consequences? Do you handle your phone any differently now? How might the calls you receive on your phone serve as an object lesson for responding to the callings of the Holy Spirit?

2. Which of these responses would best represent you if you were in the shoes of the rich young ruler whom Jesus asked to sell everything?

- I always knew this religious stuff was nuts; get me out of here!
- *Everything* everything? Even the house? The car? My favorite thing?
- Jesus, you don't understand how much I've already sacrificed; this isn't fair.
- I can't believe I just walked away from *Jesus* ... would He take me if I went back now?

3. Jesus said, "When someone has been given much, much will be required in return" (Luke 12:48). Do you agree that it can be dangerous to be rich? If so, in what areas are you most in danger?

4. Do you have regrets from missing past opportunities to answer God's callings? How can that remorse turn into motivation for future callings?

Chapter 8

———

GOD'S OWN
ADVENTURE

When I reflect on my experiences as a foster parent, I'm reminded that we didn't really come up with the idea. I don't just mean that Rachael and I didn't come up with it. Welcoming someone in need into your home and offering them a place in your family is an idea that's been around for a long time. In fact, we humans didn't come up with the idea at all.

King David wrote in one of his psalms of praise,

> Blessed is the one you choose and bring near,
>   to dwell in your courts!
> We shall be satisfied with the goodness of your
>   house,
>   the holiness of your temple! (Ps. 65:4 ESV)

David saw that the real purpose of the temple wasn't just to give the people a place to worship. Nor was it to provide a home for God, as though the Creator needed our help. Rather, the temple expressed God's plan to make a home for us—a place where we could dwell together with Him. That had been God's plan from the very beginning. He created the garden of Eden as a home for humanity, where He walked together with His creatures in the cool of the evening.

Although we have been estranged from God and separated from our home due to our sin, God has not given up on us. The Scriptures assure us that in the end, God will make all things new, heaven itself will come down to earth, and at that time, "The dwelling place of God is with man. He will dwell with them, and they will be his people, and God himself will be with them as their God. He will wipe away every tear from their eyes, and death shall be no more, neither shall there be mourning, nor crying, nor pain anymore, for the former things have passed away" (Rev. 21:3–4 ESV).

All of human history has been the working out of God's plan to adopt us as sons and daughters into His own family, to bring us back into His home. "God decided in advance to adopt us into his own family by bringing us to himself through Jesus Christ. This is what he wanted to do, and it gave him great plea-sure" (Eph. 1:5). It was for this purpose that God sent His Son into the world to take on human flesh: "But to all who believed him and accepted him, he gave the right to become children of God" (John 1:12). It was to continue this same plan that God sent the Holy Spirit into the world: "So you have not received a spirit that makes you fearful slaves. Instead, you received God's

Spirit when he adopted you as his own children. Now we call him, 'Abba, Father'" (Rom. 8:15).

MORE TO GIVE

Why did God do it? Theologians sometimes speculate about why God created the world at all. It's a pretty abstract topic—how can we even begin to imagine what God was doing and thinking before there was even time or space? Nevertheless, it's a curious thing to think about. After all, it's not as though God needed the world to exist. He was complete in and of Himself. Nor was God lonely; there has always been an infinite circle of love within the Trinity: Father, Son, and Holy Spirit. The best answer we've been able to come up with is that God created the world because He had more love to give. In other words, God had a Life Gift.

If you think about it, all the promises of the adventure are modeled first and best by God Himself through Jesus Christ:

> **1. You have a gift only you can give.** "For this is how God loved the world: He gave his one and only Son, so that everyone who believes in him will not perish but have eternal life" (John 3:16).
> **2. Someone has a need only you can meet.** "For everyone has sinned; we all fall short of God's glorious standard. Yet God, in his grace, freely makes us right in his sight. He did this

through Christ Jesus when he freed us from the penalty for our sins" (Rom. 3:23–24).

3. Joy is the journey where the gift and the need collide. "Looking to Jesus, the founder and perfecter of our faith, who for the joy that was set before him endured the cross, despising the shame, and is seated at the right hand of the throne of God" (Heb. 12:2 ESV).

4. The journey will break you … but it will also make you. "He [Christ Jesus] humbled himself in obedience to God and died a criminal's death on a cross. Therefore, God elevated him to the place of highest honor and gave him the name above all other names, that at the name of Jesus every knee should bow, in heaven and on earth and under the earth, and every tongue declare that Jesus Christ is Lord, to the glory of God the Father" (Phil. 2:8–11).

POURED OUT

One of the most amazing things we are told about Jesus in the New Testament is that He "empties" Himself. It's there in Philippians chapter 2, right before the passage I quoted above. Though God the Son was in every way equal with God the Father in power and authority, Jesus willingly chose to empty

Himself of His divine rights and privileges to take on human form, to live with all the limitations of our mortal state, and to suffer and die on our behalf. The point isn't that this was some temporary glitch where God was forced to become human in order to work out a way to save us from sin and death. The point is, this is who God really is, at the core of His being—a God who empties Himself, who pours Himself out for His creation. His power and wisdom and might are great and awesome, but even greater is His love. It was love that made the world, and love that rescued it. God's love is His highest joy.

We don't often think of the joy that God experiences in bringing us to salvation. But joy is the natural by-product of love. Because God loves, He gives. In giving, He meets our need. In meeting our need, His joy is made complete. The author of Hebrews wrote that we should be "looking to Jesus the pioneer and perfecter of our faith, who *for the sake of the joy that was set before him* endured the cross, disregarding its shame, and has taken his seat at the right hand of the throne of God" (Hebrews 12:2 NRSV).

And here's the thing: because God takes joy in sharing His love with us, He also wants us to share in His joy—not only by receiving His love, but by learning to share His love as well. When God commands us to love one another, it's not just some rule He came up with to make us obey. It's His great secret to finding true joy, and He wants to share it with us. Here's how Jesus said it:

I have loved you even as the Father has loved me. Remain in my love. When you obey my commandments, you remain in my love, just as I obey my Father's commandments and remain in his love. I have told you these things so that you will be filled with my joy. Yes, your joy will overflow! This is my commandment: Love each other in the same way I have loved you. (John 15:9–12)

When you discover your calling and give your gift to meet the need of the world, even to the point that it breaks you and remakes you, you're not just doing something *for* God. You are becoming *like* God. You are, in fact, becoming one with God, sharing in His very nature. "We know how much God loves us, and we have put our trust in his love. God is love, and all who live in love live in God, and God lives in them" (1 John 4:16). That's deep stuff.

People talk about having a bucket list of things they want to do before they die: places they want to go, people they want to meet, experiences they want to enjoy. I believe God has a different kind of bucket list for each of us, and it is far better than any list we could come up with. It is the list of experiences that are unlocked when we answer God's call. He has places He wants us to go, people He wants us to meet, and relationships He wants us to build. Many of them are not things that we would ever choose on our own with our limited understanding. Only as we enter into them in obedience do we discover how much joy they will bring to our lives.

God doesn't reveal the whole list to us all at once; rather, each step in the journey is revealed gradually as we continue to follow Jesus daily by faith. In the end, however, this bucket list is our personalized prescription for fully knowing the love of God. No experience could be greater than that, and nothing can ever take it away from us.

> But in all these things we overwhelmingly conquer through Him who loved us. For I am convinced that neither death, nor life, nor angels, nor principalities, nor things present, nor things to come, nor powers, nor height, nor depth, nor any other created thing, will be able to separate us from the love of God, which is in Christ Jesus our Lord. (Rom. 8:37–39 NASB)

AN OCEAN OF LOVE

When I remember back to that day, sitting beside the ocean, looking at that empty bucket, realizing I had something to give, I had no idea how much of a gift God was giving to me. I gave one empty bucket. God gave me back the ocean!

I know He wants to give that same love to you. And I know it will be better than you can imagine.

Could we with ink the ocean fill,
And were the skies of parchment made;
Were every stalk on earth a quill,
And every man a scribe by trade;
To write the love of God above
Would drain the ocean dry;
Nor could the scroll contain the whole,
Though stretched from sky to sky.[1]

DISCUSSION QUESTIONS

1. What is your strongest memory of feeling at home? A holiday tradition? A special family memory? Or has the feeling of home, safety, and belonging eluded you?

2. "God decided in advance to adopt us into his own family by bringing us to himself through Jesus Christ. This is what he wanted to do, and it gave him great pleasure" (Eph. 1:5). Picture Jesus standing in the open doorway of a house, His house. You are standing outside. Because of His death, burial, and resurrection, Jesus has made a place for you in God's family. Picture His nail-scarred hands reaching out to offer you a certificate of adoption that says you will be God's son or God's daughter. All you have to do is accept that certificate from Him to come inside the house and belong there forever. Have you accepted your adoption? If not, would you be willing to believe God's good news and accept adoption into His family today?

3. God always goes first. In the church, sometimes we focus on our actions toward God: we believe, we pray, we worship, we obey, we serve, we give. How might it change our perspective to remember that we never do any of these things without God first acting to give to us first? Describe how you might enter into worship differently this Sunday by first remembering that worship is God's act of giving Himself to you through Jesus Christ, by the power of the Holy Spirit.

4. Have you ever experienced an adventure, and you couldn't wait to go back and take a child, a spouse, or a friend with you so that that person could experience the adventure too? What adventure is God inviting you to take with Him in the world today?

5. What's the biggest lesson God has taught you through reading this book? Who does God want you to share that lesson with this week?

NOTES

Chapter 1: Better Than I Could Imagine

1. Not his real name. For legal and security reasons, the identities of children in the foster care system are kept private.

2. David Crowder Band, "How He Loves," *Church Music* (Sparrow Records, 2009).

Chapter 2: You Have a Gift Only You Can Give

1. Amy J. Sindler, Nancy S. Wellman, and Oren B. Stier, "Holocaust Survivors Report Long-Term Effects on Attitudes toward Food," *Journal of Nutrition Education and Behavior* 36, no 4 (2004): 189–96.

2. You can learn more about Annie's story at www.hookersforjesus.net.

Chapter 3: Someone Has a Need Only You Can Meet

1. The story is attributed by some to a Rebbe Haim of Romshishok, but no one seems to know for certain. See Marc Gellman, "Famous Spiritual Story Varies among Faiths and Cultures, but Carries the Same Message," *Chicago Tribune*, August 23, 2012, http://articles .chicagotribune.com/2012-08-23/features/sns-201208221330 --tms--godsqudctngs-a20120823-20120823_1_remarkable -story-heaven-text.

2. Thomas Merton, *No Man Is an Island* (New York: Harcourt, 1955), xxii.

3. Andy Stanley, "One, Not Everyone," (sermon, North Point Community Church, Alpharetta, GA, January 2, 2011).

Chapter 4: Joy Is the Journey Where the Gift and the Need Collide

1. Frederick Buechner, *Wishful Thinking: A Theological ABC* (New York: HarperCollins, 1973), 95.

2. Donald S. Whitney, *Spiritual Disciplines for the Christian Life* (Colorado Springs, CO: NavPress, 2014), 293.

Chapter 5: The Journey That Breaks You Will Also Make You

1. C. S. Lewis, *The Four Loves*, Harcourt Brace Modern Classics Reprint (New York: Harcourt, Brace, 1991), 121.

Chapter 6: The Community of the Called

1. For much more on this topic, I encourage all Christians and especially church leaders to read *Toxic Charity* and *When Helping Hurts* as an introduction to charitable work that supports relationships rather than unintentionally tearing them down.

Chapter 7: Missed Calls

1. See Malcolm Gladwell, "Teresa DeBrito," chap. 2 in *David and Goliath: Underdogs, Misfits, and the Art of Battling Giants* (New York: Little, Brown, 2013).

Chapter 8: God's Own Adventure

1. Frederick Martin Lehman, "The Love of God," hymn (Hope Publishing, 1917).

BIBLE CREDITS

"MY LIFE GIFT" COMMUNITY PAGE

Want to share about how you have seen God use you and your Life Gift? Want to see how God is using the Life Gifts of others around the country and around the world?

Share your Life Gift stories at **www.facebook.com/betterthanyoucanimagine** and see how God is moving in the lives of others as well!

Available in print and digital editions
everywhere books are sold

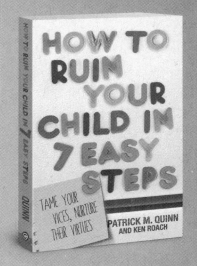